SCHOLASTIC

SUMMER EXPRESS

BETWEEN GRADES 4 & 5

W9-AVC-001

NEW YORK • TORONTO • LONDON • AUCKLAND • SYDNEY
MEXICO CITY • NEW DELHI • HONG KONG • BUENOS AIRES

Cover design by Brian LaRossa
Cover photo © Mike Powell/Gettyimages
Interior illustrations by Robert Alley, Abbey Carter, Maxie Chambliss, Sue Dennen, Shelley Dieterichs, Jane Dippold, Julie Durrell, Rusty Fletcher, James Hale, Mike Moran, Sherry Neidigh, Cary Pillo, Carol Tiernon, and Lynn Vineyard

ISBN-13 978-0-545-22694-3 / ISBN-10 0-545-22694-5
Copyright © 2010 by Scholastic Inc. All rights reserved. Printed in the U.S.A.

13 14 15 16 17 18 19 20 21 22   08   20 19 18 17 16 15

Table of Contents

Dear Parent:

Congratulations! You hold in your hands an exceptional educational tool that will give your child a head start into the coming school year.

Inside this book, you'll find one hundred practice pages that will help your child review and learn math, reading, writing, grammar, vocabulary, and so much more! The workbook is divided into 10 weeks, with two practice pages for each day of the week, Monday to Friday. However, feel free to use the pages in any order that your child would like. Here are other features you'll find inside:

- A weekly **incentive chart** and **certificate** to motivate and reward your child for his or her efforts.

- A sheet of **colorful stickers**. There are small stickers to reward your child for each day's work as well as a large sticker for completing the activities each week.

- Suggestions for fun, creative **learning activities** you can do with your child each week.

- A **recommended reading list** of age-appropriate books that you and your child can read throughout the summer.

- A **certificate of completion** to celebrate your child's accomplishments.

We hope you and your child will have a lot of fun as you work together to complete this workbook.

Enjoy!
The editors

Terrific Tips for Using This Book

1 Pick a good time for your child to work on the activities. You may want to do it around mid-morning or early afternoon when your child is not too tired.

2 Make sure your child has all the supplies he or she needs, such as pencils and markers. Set aside a special place for your child to work.

3 At the beginning of each week, discuss with your child how many minutes a day he or she would like to read. Write the goal at the top of the incentive chart for the week. (We recommend that a child entering fifth grade read at least 30 minutes a day.)

4 Reward your child's efforts with the small stickers at the end of each day. As an added bonus, let your child affix a large sticker at the bottom of the incentive chart for completing the activities each week.

5 Encourage your child to complete the worksheet, but don't force the issue. While you may want to ensure that your child succeeds, it's also important that your child maintain a positive and relaxed attitude toward school and learning.

6 After you've given your child a few minutes to look over the practice pages he or she will be working on, ask your child to tell you his or her plan of action: "Tell me about what we're doing on these pages." Hearing the explanation aloud can provide you with insights into your child's thinking processes. Can he or she complete the work independently? With guidance? If your child needs support from a family member, try offering choices regarding with whom he or she will be working. Providing choices is an approach that can help boost your child's confidence and help him or her feel more ownership of the work to be done.

7 When your child has finished the workbook, present him or her with the certificate of completion on page 143. Feel free to frame or laminate the certificate and display it on the wall for everyone to see. Your child will be so proud!

Skill-Building Activities for Any Time

The following activities are designed to complement the ten weeks of practice pages in this book. These activities don't take more than a few minutes to complete and are just a handful of ways in which you can enrich and enliven your child's learning. Use the activities to take advantage of the time you might ordinarily disregard—for example, standing in line or waiting at a bus stop. You'll be working to practice key skills and have fun together at the same time.

Finding Real-Life Connections

One of the reasons for schooling is to help children function out in the real world, to empower them with the abilities they'll truly need. So why not put those developing skills into action by enlisting your child's help with reading a map, following a recipe, checking grocery receipts, and so on. He or she can apply reading, writing, science, and math skills in important and practical ways, connecting what he or she is learning with everyday tasks.

An Eye for Patterns

A red-brick sidewalk, a beaded necklace, a Sunday newspaper—all show evidence of structure and organization. You can help your child recognize something's structure or organization by observing and talking about patterns they see. Your child will apply his or her developing ability to spot patterns across all school subject areas, including alphabet letter formation (writing), attributes of shapes and solids (geometry), and characteristics of narrative stories (reading). Being able to notice patterns is a skill shared by effective readers and writers, scientists, and mathematicians.

Journals as Learning Tools

Most of us associate journal writing with reading comprehension, but having your child keep a journal can help you keep up with his or her developing skills in other academic areas as well—from adding fractions to combining sentences. To get started, provide your child with several sheets of paper, folded in half, and stapled together. Explain that he or she will be writing and/or drawing in the journal to complement the practice pages completed each week. The journal is another tool you both can use to monitor progress of skills newly learned or practiced, or those that need improvement. Before moving on to another set of practice pages, take a few minutes to read and discuss that week's journal entries together.

Promote Reading at Home

◆ Let your child catch you in the act of reading for pleasure, whether you like reading science fiction novels or do-it-yourself magazines. Store them someplace that encourages you to read in front of your child and **demonstrate that reading is an activity you enjoy**. For example, locate your reading materials on the coffee table instead of your nightstand.

◆ Set aside a family reading time. By designating a reading time each week, your family is assured an opportunity to discuss with each other what you're reading. You can, for example, share a funny quote from an article. Or your child can tell you his or her favorite part of a story. The key is to **make a family tradition of reading and sharing books** of all kinds together.

◆ **Put together collections of reading materials** your child can access easily. Gather them in baskets or bins that you can place in the family room, the car, and your child's bedroom. You can refresh your child's library by borrowing materials from your community's library, buying used books, or swapping books and magazines with friends and neighbors.

Skills Review and Practice

Educators have established learning standards for math and language arts. Listed below are some of the important skills covered in *Summer Express* that will help your child review and prepare for the coming school year so that he or she is better prepared to meet these learning standards.

Math

Skills Your Child Will Review	Skills Your Child Will Practice to Prepare for Grade Five
◆ adding without regrouping multiplication facts	◆ solving word problems using knowledge of money values and decimals
◆ finding area and perimeter (feet, yards)	◆ solving word problems using multiplication skills
◆ reading tables, charts, and bar graphs	◆ identifying equivalent fractions
	◆ adding with regrouping
	◆ adding decimals (e.g., money values)
	◆ subtracting with regrouping and multiple regrouping
	◆ subtracting fractions
	◆ multiplying with regrouping
	◆ multiplying decimals and whole numbers
	◆ dividing with remainders and decimals
	◆ changing decimals to fractions
	◆ plotting coordinates on a grid
	◆ matching geometric terms with corresponding shapes
	◆ recognizing equivalent decimals, fractions, and percents

Language Arts

Skills Your Child Will Review	Skills Your Child Will Practice to Prepare for Grade Five
◆ proofreading (e.g., grammar, meaning, spelling, sentence variety)	◆ using proofreading symbols (e.g., capitalization, missing words)
◆ prewriting strategies to relate information (e.g., graphic organizers)	◆ using a graphic organizer to write a concrete poem
◆ writing for a purpose (e.g., expository paragraph, persuasive paragraph, descriptive paragraph)	◆ writing for a purpose (e.g., comparison paragraph)
◆ expanding and combining sentences	◆ identifying incomplete sentences
◆ identifying topic sentences	◆ fixing run-on sentences
◆ writing in paragraph form	◆ adding details to increase a reader's interest
◆ using parts of speech	◆ using exact verbs to clarify meaning
◆ writing in upper- and lowercase cursive letters	◆ identifying parts of a paragraph
◆ demonstrating knowledge of level-appropriate reading vocabulary (e.g., synonyms, antonyms, and so on)	◆ identifying parts of speech (e.g., present-, past-, and future-tense verbs)
	◆ using subject-verb agreement
	◆ punctuating using commas and colons
	◆ using supporting details
	◆ summarizing information
	◆ using phonetic, structural, and context analysis (e.g., syllables) to identify unfamiliar words

Helping Your Child Get Ready: Week 1

These are the skills your child will be working on this week.

Math
- adding without regrouping
- adding with regrouping

Reading
- sequencing

Writing
- including details

Vocabulary
- synonyms and antonyms
- idioms

Grammar
- sentence types

Handwriting
- uppercase cursive letters

Here are some activities you and your child might enjoy.

Restaurant Review Next time you eat out, have your child write a review of the restaurant. Encourage him or her to use lots of descriptive words.

Secret Messages Suggest that your child come up with a code to write secret messages in. Have him or her trade messages with you or another family member.

Word Problem Reversals To help your child understand tricky word problems, have him or her work in reverse! Supply a number sentence such as $5 \times 8 = 40$ or $40 \div 5 = 8$ and have your child come up with a word problem for it.

Set a Summer's End Goal Suggest that your child set a goal for the end of the summer. Perhaps it's becoming an expert on a favorite animal, or learning how to count in another language. Help your child come up with a plan for success.

Your child might enjoy reading the following books:

Frindle
by Andrew Clements

Afternoon of the Elves
by Janet Taylor Lisle

The Dream Keeper and Other Poems
by Langston Hughes

Goals:
1. Read 5 Books
2. Go to library
3. Learn to dive
4. Build a treehouse
5. Learn a magic trick

Special Note: The activity for Day 5 of this week is a mini-book. Have your child tear out the page along the perforation and cut along the dotted line. After positioning the two sections so the mini-book pages are in sequence, your child can staple and fold to form a book. Then he or she can answer all the puzzles in the mini-book.

_____
Name Here

's Incentive Chart: Week 1

This week, I plan to read _____ minutes each day.

CHART YOUR PROGRESS HERE.

Week 1	Day 1	Day 2	Day 3	Day 4	Day 5
I read for...	minutes	minutes	minutes	minutes	minutes
Put a sticker to show you completed each day's work.					

Congratulations!

Wow! You did a great job this week!

#1

Place sticker here.

Parent or Caregiver's Signature _____

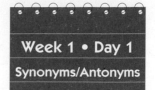
Two Left Feet

These shoes are all mixed up! You can pair them off. Each shoe contains a word that is a synonym for a word on another shoe. Synonyms are words that have the same or almost the same meaning. Put each pair of shoes together by coloring them the same color. Use a different color for each pair.

sensible   popular   enormous   rich

wealthy   good-looking   primitive   massive

early   reasonable   favorite   attractive

Lace up those synonym shoes! Each of the shoelaces has a word that is an antonym for a pair of shoes above. Antonyms are words that have the opposite meanings. Color each lace the same color as the pair of shoes that is its opposite.

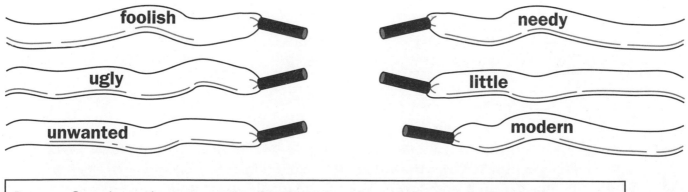

foolish   needy

ugly   little

unwanted   modern

Bonus: Create antonym *socks*. Challenge a friend to match them to the shoes.

Climbing High

To add multiple-digit numbers without regrouping, follow these steps.
1. Add the ones column.
2. Add the tens column.
3. Add the hundreds column.
4. Continue working through each column in order.

Add.

A.
$$\begin{array}{r} 1,136 \\ + \ 2,433 \\ \hline \end{array}$$
$$\begin{array}{r} 9,025 \\ + \ 851 \\ \hline \\ - \end{array}$$

B.
$$\begin{array}{r} 8,730 \\ + \ 1,252 \\ \hline \\ - \end{array}$$
$$\begin{array}{r} 2,928 \\ + \ 5,021 \\ \hline \end{array}$$
$$\begin{array}{r} 3,650 \\ + \ 4,210 \\ \hline \end{array}$$
$$\begin{array}{r} 80,662 \\ + \ 11,136 \\ \hline \end{array}$$

C.
$$\begin{array}{r} 55,100 \\ + \ 31,892 \\ \hline \\ - \end{array}$$
$$\begin{array}{r} 60,439 \\ + \ 30,310 \\ \hline \end{array}$$
$$\begin{array}{r} 81,763 \\ + \ 8,231 \\ \hline \end{array}$$
$$\begin{array}{r} 36,034 \\ + \ 41,753 \\ \hline \end{array}$$

D.
$$\begin{array}{r} 321,957 \\ + \ 260,041 \\ \hline \\ - \end{array}$$
$$\begin{array}{r} 623,421 \\ + \ 151,441 \\ \hline \end{array}$$
$$\begin{array}{r} 264,870 \\ + \ 303,120 \\ \hline \end{array}$$
$$\begin{array}{r} 592,604 \\ + \ 102,335 \\ \hline \end{array}$$
$$\begin{array}{r} 127,094 \\ + \ 832,502 \\ \hline \\ - \end{array}$$

Mount Everest is the highest mountain in the world. To find the height of Mount Everest, begin climbing in Row D. Write the underlined numbers in order. Continue writing the numbers in Row C, Row B, and Row A. How many feet did you climb?

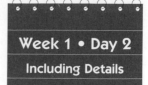

Spout Some Specifics

To be a good writer, it is important to know what you are writing about, to be specific, and to include details. All this helps to create a picture for your readers and will make your writing more interesting and informative. Compare the two phrases below. Which one is more specific, interesting, and informative? Which one creates a more vivid picture?

a vehicle or *an old, rusty, dilapidated pick-up truck with flat tires and a shattered windshield*

For each general word or phrase, write a more specific word. Then add details to describe each specific word.

Specific Word		Details
1. a body of water	_____	_____
2. a piece of furniture	_____	_____
3. an article of clothing	_____	_____
4. a child's toy	_____	_____
5. a noise or sound	_____	_____
6. a tool	_____	_____
7. a group of people	_____	_____
8. a reptile	_____	_____
9. garden plants	_____	_____
10. a kind of fruit	_____	_____
11. a kind of vegetable	_____	_____
12. a drink	_____	_____
13. footwear	_____	_____
14. musical instrument	_____	_____
15. a holiday	_____	_____

Look at yourself in the mirror. Then write on a sheet of paper as many words and phrases as you can to describe yourself so that someone who does not know you would get a clear, vivid picture of what you look like.

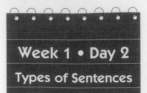

Types of Sentences

A **declarative sentence** makes a statement. An **interrogative sentence** asks a question. An **exclamatory sentence** shows strong feeling. An **imperative sentence** states a command.

A. **What kind of sentence is each of the following? Write** *declarative,* *interrogative,* *exclamatory,* **or** *imperative* **on the line.**

1. Merlin carried the baby to safety. _____

2. Why did traitors poison the town's wells? _____

3. Go back and fetch the missing sword. _____

4. Slip the sword into the groove, and pull it out. _____

5. The king was England's bravest ruler! _____

6. Who will follow Selene? _____

B. **Identify which groups of words are incomplete sentences and which are complete sentences. Write** *incomplete* **or** *complete* **on the line.**

1. Sarah at the edge of the square. _____

2. The knights fought so bravely! _____

3. How did Kay treat her dog? _____

4. The sword out of the stone. _____

5. Natalie was trained to be a pilot. _____

C. **Correct the incomplete sentences in part B. Add an action word to each one. Then rewrite the complete sentence on the line.**

1. _____

2. _____

Scholastic Inc.   *Summer Express: Between Grades 4 & 5*

A Real Cool Cowboy

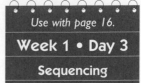

The events in a story take place in a certain order. This is the **sequence** of events.

Pecos Bill is a well-known character in American folklore. His legend developed from a magazine article written by Edward O'Reilly in 1923. This cowboy hero is often credited for being the creator of branding, roping, and other cowboy activities. It is also said that Pecos Bill taught broncos how to buck and cowboys how to ride.

Legend has it that Pecos Bill was born in the 1830s in Texas. He teethed on a bowie knife and had bears and other wild animals as friends. On a family trip to the West, little Bill fell out of the wagon near the Pecos River. He was found by coyotes that raised him.

Two famous natural landmarks are also amusingly traced back to Pecos Bill—the Grand Canyon and Death Valley. Supposedly, Pecos Bill once made a bet that he could ride an Oklahoma cyclone without a saddle. The cyclone was not able to throw him off, and it finally "rained out" under him in Arizona. This rain was so heavy that it created the Grand Canyon. When he reached California, Pecos Bill crashed. It was the force of his fall that is said to have created Death Valley. In actuality, some rocks in the deepest part of the Grand Canyon date back to about two billion years ago. The Colorado River began forming the Grand Canyon about six million years ago. Over

centuries, the water eroded the layers of rock, and the walls of the canyon were created. More erosion occurred later as a result of wind, rain, and melting snow. Death Valley is a desert in California and Nevada. It contains the lowest point in the Western Hemisphere at 282 feet below sea level.

No one is quite sure how Pecos Bill died. One version says he laughed himself to death after listening to silly questions a man from Boston asked him about the West.

1. **Look at each picture. Number the events in the order in which they happened in the story. Write a sentence for each.**

_____   _____   _____

_____   _____   _____

_____   _____   _____

_____   _____   _____

_____   _____   _____

_____   _____   _____

2. **Four words from the story are hidden in the puzzle. The definition of each word is given below. Shade in the letters for each word, reading left to right and top to bottom. The remaining letters will spell the name of a real cool cowboy two times.**

   a piece of writing

   laughingly

   attributed with

   a particular form of something

a	p	r	t	e	i	c
c	o	l	e	s	a	b
m	u	s	i	i	n	l
g	l	y	l	c	p	r
e	d	e	i	t	c	e
o	d	v	s	e	b	r
i	s	l	l	i	o	n

Read a story about an imaginary character. On another sheet of paper, write five events from the character's life in the order in which they happened.

Wild Birds

Some addition problems will require regrouping several times. The steps look like this.

1. Add the ones column. Regroup if needed.

2. Add the tens column. Regroup if needed.

3. Add the hundreds column. Regroup if needed.

4. Continue working through each column in order.

$$
\begin{array}{r} 1 \\ 37,462 \\ +\quad 22,798 \\ \hline 0 \end{array}
\qquad
\begin{array}{r} 11 \\ 37,462 \\ +\quad 22,798 \\ \hline 60 \end{array}
\qquad
\begin{array}{r} 111 \\ 37,462 \\ +\quad 22,798 \\ \hline 260 \end{array}
\qquad
\begin{array}{r} 111 \\ 37,462 \\ +\quad 22,798 \\ \hline 60,260 \end{array}
$$

Add. Then use the code to finish the fun fact below.

bald eagle

Z. 953 + 418   B. 295 + 337   R. 418 + 793   Q. 565 + 957   S. 862 + 339   X. 478 + 283

falcon

I. 2,428 + 6,679   C. 1,566 + 2,487   Y. 3,737 + 6,418   A. 9,289 + 4,735   Y. 8,754 + 368

vulture

L. 57,854 + 45,614   P. 29,484 + 46,592   E. 36,238 + 46,135   F. 67,139 + 25,089

owl

D. 240,669 + 298,727   O. 476,381 + 175,570   R. 882,948 + 176,524

What do all of these birds have in common?

They are _____ _____ _____ _____ _____   _____ _____
632   9,107   1,211   539,396   1,201   651,951   92,228

_____ _____ _____ _____ .
76,076   1,059,472   82,373   10,155

Letter Match

Match the cursive letters to their partners.

Cursive		Print		Cursive		Print
$\mathcal{F}$		A		$\mathcal{R}$		N
$\mathcal{J}$		B		$\mathcal{Y}$		O
$\mathcal{B}$		C		$\mathcal{V}$		P
$\mathcal{L}$		D		$\mathcal{P}$		Q
$\mathcal{A}$		E		$\mathcal{N}$		R
$\mathcal{H}$		F		$\mathcal{S}$		S
$\mathcal{E}$		G		$\mathcal{Q}$		T
$\mathcal{K}$		H		$\mathcal{Y}$		U
$\mathcal{D}$		I		$\mathcal{X}$		V
$\mathcal{M}$		J		$\mathcal{W}$		W
$\mathcal{I}$		K		$\mathcal{U}$		X
$\mathcal{G}$		L		$\mathcal{O}$		Y
$\mathcal{C}$		M		$\mathcal{T}$		Z

18

Foods

Foods Complete each of these idioms by putting the name of a food on each blank. If you don't know the idiom, put in your best guess.

be a couch _____ (sit around, be lazy)

walk on _____ (be very cautious)

in a _____ (have a big problem)

spill the _____ (give away a secret)

a piece of _____ (something that's very easy)

like two _____ in a pod (to be very similar)

go _____ (go crazy)

3

Eating Your Words

To "eat your words" is an expression called an idiom. Idioms can't be taken literally. To understand them, you have to know their special meanings.

Lucy said we'd lose the game, but we won. Now she'll have to eat her words.

Name

Similes

Similes Expressions that compare two things using the words "as" or "like" are called similes. Complete each of these popular similes by putting the name of an animal on each blank. If you don't know the simile, put in your best guess.

as wise as a/an _____

as proud as a/an _____

as sly as a/an _____

as busy as a/an _____

as graceful as a/an _____

as strong as a/an _____

as quiet as a/an _____

as stubborn as a/an _____

as gentle as a/an _____

6

Draw a picture that illustrates the meaning of one of the idioms in this mini-book. Write the idiom at the bottom of the page.

_____
_____

8

Parts of the Body

Complete each of the idioms on these two pages by putting the name of a part of the body on each blank. If you don't know the idiom, put in your best guess.

be all _____ (be eager to listen)

hold your _____ (be silent)

have your _____ in the clouds (to daydream)

make your _____ water (look and smell tasty)

get it off your _____ (make a confession)

Animals

Complete each of these idioms by putting the name of an animal on each blank. If you don't know the idiom, put in your best guess.

have a _____ in your throat (be hoarse)

raining _____ and _____ (rain hard)

be a _____ (feel fearful or anxious)

have _____ in your stomach (feel nervous)

smell a _____ (suspect something's wrong)

_____ around (play noisily)

have _____ in your pants (feel restless)

Scholastic Inc.   Summer Express: Between Grades 4 & 5

---

get a pat on your _____ (be praised)

make your _____ stand on end (be scary)

be all _____ (be awkward or clumsy)

stick your _____ out (take a risk)

button your _____ (keep quiet)

pull someone's _____ (fool someone)

catch your _____ (be noticed)

on your _____ (be alert)

give someone a _____ (help someone)

Create your own

similes by completing each of the phrases below. Try to make your similes as descriptive as possible.

as funny as _____

as noisy as _____

as scary as _____

as fast as _____

as playful as _____

as angry as _____

Helping Your Child Get Ready: Week 2

These are the skills your child will be working on this week.

Math
- rounding and estimating
- reading tables and charts
- word problems

Reading
- following directions

Writing
- elaborating
- combining sentences

Vocabulary
- compound words

Grammar
- parts of speech
- commas

Here are some activities you and your child might enjoy.

Fantastic Stats Your child can use a calculator to create fantastic stats about him- or herself. For instance, have your child figure out how many times he or she has breathed since birth. Here's how:

1. Figure out a breath rate for one minute. **2.** Find how many breaths in one hour (multiply by 60). **3.** Find how many breaths in 1 day (multiply breaths per hour by 24). **4.** Find how many breaths in one year (multiply breaths per day by 365). **5.** Find how many breaths in the n years he or she has been alive (multiply breaths per year by n).

30-Second Rhyme-Around Give your child 30 seconds to think of as many rhymes as possible for a given word. Start off with words that are easier to rhyme (like *cat*), and work up to more challenging ones.

Word Expert Boost your child's vocabulary by playing Word Expert. Tell him or her that for each word you say, he or she must give you an antonym, a synonym, and an example of the word. For example, for *awesome*, a synonym might be *amazing*, an antonym might be *terrible*, and an example could be the *Grand Canyon*.

Family Newsletter Encourage your budding journalist by having him or her write a family newsletter. It can include news, weather reports, movie and book reviews, upcoming events, and even advertisements.

Your child might enjoy reading the following books:

A Single Shard
by Linda Sue Park

I, Juan de Pareja
by Elizabeth Borton de Trevino

Shiloh
by Phyllis Reynolds Naylor

LILLIAN'S NEWSLETTER

Today's News

Movie Review

Book Review

_____'s Incentive Chart: Week 2

Name Here

This week, I plan to read _____ minutes each day.

CHART YOUR PROGRESS HERE.

Week 1	Day 1	Day 2	Day 3	Day 4	Day 5
I read for...	minutes	minutes	minutes	minutes	minutes
Put a sticker to show you completed each day's work.					

Congratulations!

Wow! You did a great job this week!

#1

Place sticker here.

Parent or Caregiver's Signature _____

Bee Riddle

Riddle: What did the farmer get when he tried to reach the beehive?

Round each number. Then use the Decoder to solve the riddle by filling in the spaces at the bottom of the page.

1. Round 7 to the nearest ten _____
2. Round 23 to the nearest ten _____
3. Round 46 to the nearest ten _____
4. Round 92 to the nearest ten _____
5. Round 203 to the nearest hundred _____
6. Round 420 to the nearest hundred _____
7. Round 588 to the nearest hundred _____
8. Round 312 to the nearest hundred _____
9. Round 549 to the nearest hundred _____
10. Round 710 to the nearest hundred _____

Decoder

400............ **A**
800............ **W**
30.............. **O**
10.............. **Y**
25.............. **E**
500............ **I**
210............ **J**
20.............. **L**
40.............. **C**
700............ **U**
90.............. **S**
100............ **T**
600............ **G**
95.............. **F**
50.............. **N**
550............ **V**
300............ **Z**
7................ **H**
200............ **Z**

A "B __ __ __ __"   __ __ __ __ __ __
    10 5 8 1   4 9 7 3 6 2

Make It Interesting

A sentence can be very simple. This sentence tells who did what.

The crew worked.

As you write and revise your writing, add details about people, places, or things, or about where, when, and what happens. This will make your writing more interesting. Here's how the sentence above was revised several times. Each sentence gives a little more information.

The construction crew worked.
The construction crew worked quickly.
The construction crew worked quickly to clear the rubble.
The construction crew worked quickly to clear the rubble at the building site.
The construction crew worked quickly yesterday to clear the rubble at the building site.

Rewrite each sentence four times. Add new details each time to tell more about whom or what, how, where, and when.

The children played.

1. _____

_____

2. _____

_____

3. _____

_____

4. _____

_____

A package arrived.

1. _____

_____

2. _____

_____

3. _____

_____

4. _____

_____

Rewrite the following sentence several times on a sheet of paper. Remove a detail each time until you are left with a very simple sentence.

The excited team cheered wildly after winning the championship basketball game.

Green Gift

"Poor Grandma! I wish there was some way we could cheer her up," Amy said to her brother Mark.

Grandma had fallen and broken her leg. The doctor said she would be in a cast for six weeks. Grandma was very active and loved to work in her garden, so she would not enjoy sitting in her chair waiting for her leg to heal.

"I have an idea," said Mark. "I saw some pictures of terrariums in a magazine. Terrariums are little indoor gardens that can be grown in glass jars. Let's make a terrarium for Grandma, so she can enjoy a garden in her house."

Amy thought Mark had a great idea, so the two of them found the magazine article with the directions for making a terrarium and showed their mom. She agreed that a terrarium would be a perfect gift for Grandma. She helped Amy and Mark find a large, clear glass bottle, which they cleaned and checked for leaks. After a trip to the garden shop to buy the materials, they were ready to assemble the terrarium.

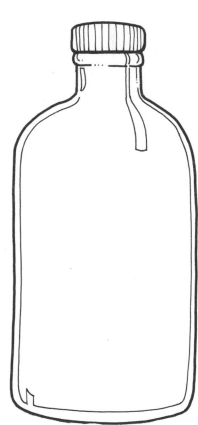

First, they put a small layer of charcoal and gravel drainage material at the bottom of the bottle. This would keep the soil from getting too damp.

Draw a layer of charcoal and gravel at the bottom of the bottle.

Next, they added a layer of dark, rich soil.

Draw a layer of dark soil on top of the drainage materials.

Now they were ready to add the plants. Mark used a long-handled spoon to tap out holes in the soil. Amy had chosen two plants at the garden shop. One was tall with long, thin, green leaves. The other was short with bright pink flowers. Mark placed the plants in the holes and gently tapped the soil down over their roots.

Draw the two plants Mark and Amy planted.

To make the terrarium even more colorful, Amy placed some colorful rocks and bright green moss around the plants.

Draw the colorful rocks and green moss that Amy added to the terrarium.

Finally, Mark and Amy lightly watered the plants by pouring water through a small funnel at the top of the bottle. Now the terrarium was ready to take to Grandma.

When Amy and Mark showed Grandma her new terrarium, she was so happy. Now she had a beautiful little garden to enjoy right inside her home.

Mark and Amy want to make another terrarium for their Aunt Hilda's birthday, but they lost the magazine article with the directions. Help them make a new set of directions.

1. Make a list of all the materials Mark and Amy needed to assemble the terrarium.

   _____

   _____

   _____

2. What must be done to the bottle before adding the materials to it? _____

   _____

3. Tell how to assemble the terrarium. Be sure to use the steps in correct order.

   First, _____

   _____

   Next, add _____

   Now use a long-handled spoon to_____

      and then add _____

      and tap_____

   To make the terrarium more colorful, place _____

   _____

   Finally, _____

   _____

4. Why do you think Amy only chose two plants for the terrarium?_____

   _____

   _____

5. What kinds of plants would not be good choices for a terrarium? _____

   _____

26

Cut a label off a product your family is finished using. On another sheet of paper, write three questions involving the directions on the label for using the product. Give the label and the questions to someone in your family to answer.

How's Your Heart Rate?

You Need:
◆ stopwatch or watch with a second hand   ◆ tennis ball

Animals have hearts that do the same job as a person's heart. An animal's heart beats to pump blood through its body. What's different about an animal heart and a human heart? The number of times it beats in a minute.

Each day your heart beats about 100,000 times. That's enough times to pump almost 1,500 gallons of blood throughout your body! By the time you are 70 years old, your heart will have pumped about 38 million gallons of blood. No wonder it's important to keep your heart strong and healthy!

The number of times a heart beats in a certain amount of time is called **heart rate**. Check out the table to find some average animal heart rates. Then follow the steps to add your heart rate to the table.

ANIMAL	HEART RATE (for one minute)
Canary	1,000
Mouse	650
Chicken	200
Cat	110
Dog	80
Adult human	72
Giraffe	60
Tiger	45
Elephant	25
Gray whale	8
You	

How to Find Your Heart Rate

• Place two fingers on your neck or your wrist. Move them around until you feel a pulse beat.

• Count the beats for 30 seconds. Have someone at home time you with the watch.

• Multiply the number of beats by two. That number is your heart rate for one minute.

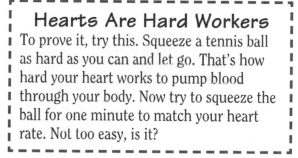

Hearts Are Hard Workers
To prove it, try this. Squeeze a tennis ball as hard as you can and let go. That's how hard your heart works to pump blood through your body. Now try to squeeze the ball for one minute to match your heart rate. Not too easy, is it?

Answer these questions about animals' heart rates, using the information on the table.

1. Which animal's heart beats fastest in one minute? _____

   Which beats slowest? _____

2. What do you notice about the size of the animal compared with its heart rate?

   _____

3. Where do you think a horse's heart rate might fit on the table? Explain your answer.

   _____

   _____

4. Which animal is your heart rate the closest to? _____

Compound It All!

 A **compound word** *is formed by combining two words.*

Each word below can be combined with one of the other words to form a compound word. Starting with *cookbook*, take the second word, *book*, and write it on the next line. Then choose a word from the box that will make a new compound word. Continue until you have used all the words in the box.

house	way	walk	side	hill
cook	store	book	hold	up

cook   +   book   =   cookbook

_____ + _____ = _____

_____ + _____ = _____

_____ + _____ = _____

_____ + _____ = _____

_____ + _____ = _____

_____ + _____ = _____

_____ + _____ = _____

_____ + _____ = _____

_____ + _____ = _____

Starting with the word *quarterback,* continue to make compound words as you did above using the words from the box.

mate	stick	back	quarter	yard	room	ball

_____ + _____ = _____

_____ + _____ = _____

_____ + _____ = _____

_____ + _____ = _____

_____ + _____ = _____

_____ + _____ = _____

Read a page from a book you are reading, a newspaper column, or a magazine article. On another sheet of paper, list the compound words you find.

28

Scholastic Inc.   Summer Express: Between Grades 4 & 5

Attack of the Massive Melon!

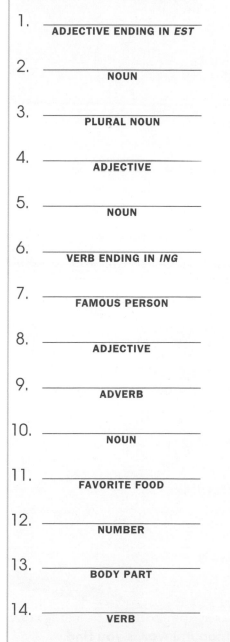

Don't read this story yet! Give it to a partner and ask him or her to tell you the parts of speech under the blanks below. You give a word for each part of speech, and your partner writes it in the blank. Then he or she writes the words in the story and reads the story aloud.

1. _____
   ADJECTIVE ENDING IN _EST_

2. _____
   NOUN

3. _____
   PLURAL NOUN

4. _____
   ADJECTIVE

5. _____
   NOUN

6. _____
   VERB ENDING IN _ING_

7. _____
   FAMOUS PERSON

8. _____
   ADJECTIVE

9. _____
   ADVERB

10. _____
    NOUN

11. _____
    FAVORITE FOOD

12. _____
    NUMBER

13. _____
    BODY PART

14. _____
    VERB

I decided that I was going to grow

the _____ garden in the world. I used a
          1

_____ to dig holes in the backyard, then I
          2

spread seeds and _____ all around. Pretty
                          3

soon, my garden started looking _____ . I
                                          4

had planted _____ seeds, but a watermelon
                  5

started _____ out of the ground! It grew
                  6

and grew. This watermelon became bigger than

_____ ! Mom said we should eat it before
          7

it turned _____. So every day I climbed
                  8

_____ up a _____ , then leaped
          9   10

to the top of the melon and cut off huge pieces.

We made watermelon shakes, peanut butter and

watermelon sandwiches, and _____ with
                                          11

watermelon sauce. I've eaten almost nothing but

melon for the last _____ months! Mom
                          12

said, "Don't look a gift horse in the _____"
                                                  13

I sure learned a lesson: Don't bite off more than you

can _____ !
          14

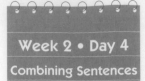
Hot Subjects

 If two sentences share the same subject, information about the subject can be written as a phrase after the subject in the new sentence. Be sure to use commas to set apart the phrase from the rest of the sentence.

Sentence 1: **The Gateway Arch is America's tallest human-made monument.**

Sentence 2: **The monument rises 630 feet above the ground.**

Combined: **The Gateway Arch, America's tallest human-made monument, rises 630 feet above the ground.**

Read the sentences. Combine the ideas in each pair into one sentence by including information in a phrase after the subject in the sentence.

1. **The Caspian Sea is the world's largest lake.**
   The lake covers an area about the same size as Montana.

   _____

2. **The Komodo dragon is a member of the monitor family.**
   It can grow to a length of 10 feet.

   _____

3. **Our closest star is the sun.**
   It is estimated to be more than 27,000,000°F.

   _____

4. **Ronald W. Reagan was our nation's 40th president.**
   He worked as a Hollywood actor for almost 30 years.

   _____

5. **Georgia is the state that grows the most peanuts.**
   It harvests over 1.3 billion pounds each year.

   _____

6. **Barry Bonds is major league baseball's all-time homerun hitter.**
   He broke Hank Aaron's record in 2007.

   _____

A Penny Saved Is a Penny Earned

Write a number sentence for each problem. Solve.

A. Aimee and her 2 sisters are saving to buy a camera. Aimee has $12.89. Each of her sisters has $28.53. How much money do all the girls have combined?	**B.** Katie has $23.95 in her purse, $17.23 in her bank, and $76.82 in her savings account. What is the total amount of Katie's money?
C. Jonah worked in the yard for 3 days. The first day he earned $7.96. The second day he earned $2.00 more than the first day. The third day he earned $2.00 less than the first day. How much did Jonah earn altogether?	**D.** Jack has $9.29. He also has 79 dimes and 139 pennies. How much money does he have altogether?
E. Kelsey has 478 coins in her collection. The silver dollars equal $79.00, and the quarters equal $99.75. How much is Kelsey's collection worth in all?	**F.** Claire bought lemonade for herself and two friends. Each cup costs $1.75. How much did Claire spend in all?

 On another sheet of paper, write a word problem with a sum equal to $41.68.

31

Triple the Fun

When you write, you may want to list three or more items or ideas in a series in a single sentence. Be sure to use a comma after each item in a series except after the last item.

Max dressed quickly, ate breakfast, and raced out the door.
Luis, Jamie, Leroy, and Sam met Max at the baseball field.
They were hopeful, excited, and nervous about their first game.

Answer each question below in a complete sentence. Use commas where they are needed. Make sure each sentence begins and ends correctly. Remember to check your spelling.

1. **What are the titles of three books you've read recently or would like to read? Remember to underline the title of each book.**

    _____

2. **What are four of the planets in our solar system closer to the sun than Pluto?**

    _____

3. **What are three green, leafy vegetables?**

    _____

4. **What countries would you like to visit? Include at least three in your answer.**

    _____

5. **What months fall between January and July?**

    _____

6. **What three things have you done today to help out at home?**

    _____

7. **What states or bodies of water border your state?**

    _____

8. **What activities do you and your friends enjoy in the summer?**

    _____

9. **Who are some of the most important people in your life?**

    _____

Make up some questions like the ones above and challenge someone you know to answer them on a sheet of paper. Correct the sentences.

Scholastic Inc.   Summer Express: Between Grades 4 & 5

Helping Your Child Get Ready: Week 3

These are the skills your child will be working on this week.

Math
- subtraction with regrouping
- subtraction with multiple regrouping

Reading
- predicting
- drawing conclusions

Writing
- combining sentences
- sentence variety

Vocabulary
- prefixes

Grammar
- proofreading

Handwriting
- lowercase cursive letters

Here are some activities you and your child might enjoy.

30-Second Synonyms Give your child 30 seconds to come up with as many synonyms as possible for the word *happy*. Then try *sad*.

Cricket Weather Can you hear crickets chirping where you live? If you can, here's a fun way to practice some math skills. Tell your child to count how many times a cricket chirps in 15 seconds. Have him or her add 37 to that number. The sum is the temperature in degrees Fahrenheit!

Fire Safety Plan Ask your child to create a fire safety plan booklet. He or she can draw a map on each page to describe how each family member should escape from your home. Another page can explain where family members should go if they need to leave the house quickly.

Set a Family Record How long can your child hop? It's time to set a family record! Have him or her choose an activity and see how long he or she can do it. Then see if he or she can break the record the next day.

Your child might enjoy reading the following books:

Tom's Midnight Garden
by Phillippa Pearce

Who Was That Masked Man, Anyway?
by Avi

Zeely
by Virginia Hamilton

_____ **'s Incentive Chart: Week 3**

Name Here

This week, I plan to read _____ minutes each day.

CHART YOUR PROGRESS HERE.

Week 1	Day 1	Day 2	Day 3	Day 4	Day 5
I read for...	minutes	minutes	minutes	minutes	minutes
Put a sticker to show you completed each day's work.					

Congratulations!

Wow! You did a great job this week!

#1

Place sticker here.

Parent or Caregiver's Signature _____

Checkmate

To subtract with regrouping, follow these steps.

1. Subtract the ones column. Regroup if needed.

```
   2 11
  4 3 1
-   2 6 6
─────────
        5
```

2. Subtract the tens column. Regroup if needed.

```
    12
  3 2 11
  4 3 1
-   2 6 6
─────────
      6 5
```

3. Subtract the hundreds column. Regroup if needed.

```
    12
  3 2 11
  4 3 1
-   2 6 6
─────────
    1 6 5
```

Subtract. Cross out the chess piece with the matching difference. The last piece standing is the winner of the match.

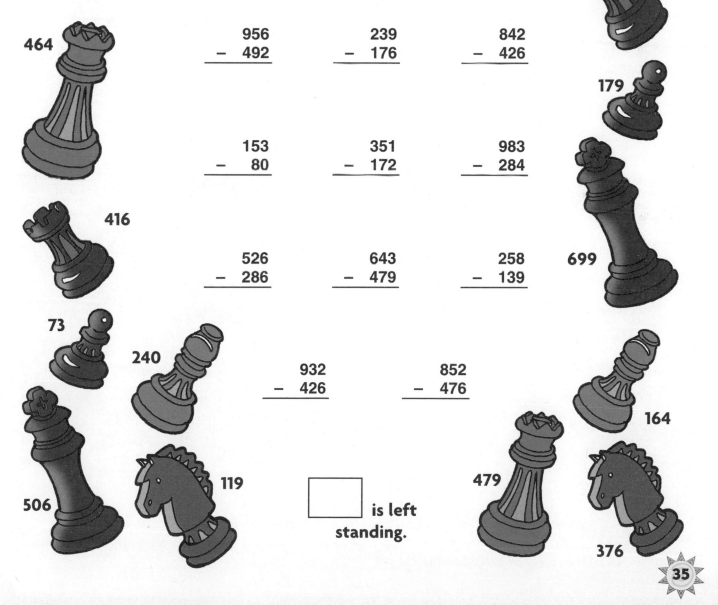

63

464

```
  956
- 492
```

```
  239
- 176
```

```
  842
- 426
```

179

```
  153
-  80
```

```
  351
- 172
```

```
  983
- 284
```

416

```
  526
- 286
```

```
  643
- 479
```

```
  258
- 139
```

699

73

240

```
  932
- 426
```

```
  852
- 476
```

164

119

___ is left standing.

479

506

376

Scholastic Inc.   Summer Express: Between Grades 4 & 5

All Aboard!

A **prefix** is a word part that is added to the beginning of a word and changes its meaning. Here are some common prefixes and their meanings.

a-	on	**multi-**	many, much	**super-**	above, beyond
anti-	against	**non-**	not	**trans-**	across
im-	not	**over-**	too much	**un-**	not
in-	not	**pre-**	before	**under-**	below, less than
inter-	among, between	**re-**	again		
mis-	wrong	**re-**	back		

Here are some words with these prefixes. Use the information from the chart to write what you think each word means. Then use a dictionary to check your definitions. Make corrections if needed.

1. **aboard** _____
2. **supervisor** _____
3. **multicolored** _____
4. **misunderstood** _____
5. **international** _____
6. **preheat** _____
7. **nonstop** _____
8. **transcontinental** _____
9. **uncomfortable** _____
10. **overpriced** _____
11. **review** _____
12. **unbelievable** _____
13. **inexpensive** _____
14. **underweight** _____
15. **impatient** _____
16. **antifreeze** _____

What other prefixes do you know? On another sheet of paper, list them along with their meanings. Knowing what a prefix means can help you to figure out the meaning of an unfamiliar word.

36

Letter Match

Match the cursive letters to their partners.

j	a	*q*	n
m	b	*w*	o
c	c	*o*	p
a	d	*z*	q
h	e	*v*	r
k	f	*p*	s
e	g	*y*	t
d	h	*s*	u
f	i	*u*	v
b	j	*n*	w
i	k	*t*	x
l	l	*r*	y
g	m	*x*	z

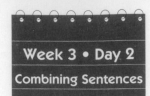

Sentence Building

When you write about something, try to include interesting details. Sometimes you can take the important details from several related sentences and add them to the main sentence.

Kyle and Jim had a great plan.
They're my brothers.
The plan was for a tree house.

Now here's a sentence that combines all the important details.

My brothers Kyle and Jim had a great plan for a tree house.

Read each group of sentences. Take the important details from the two related sentences and add them to the main sentence to make one sentence.

1. **My brothers built a tree house. They built it in the old oak tree. It's in our backyard.**

   _____

2. **Jim made a ladder for the tree house. He made it out of rope. It is sturdy.**

   _____

3. **Kyle bought paint. The paint was brown. He bought a gallon.**

   _____

4. **Kyle and Jim finished painting. They painted the walls. It took an hour.**

   _____

5. **Jim painted a sign. He painted "no trespassing." The sign is on the tree house door.**

   _____

6. **A squirrel leaped into their tree house. It leaped from a branch. It was curious.**

   _____

7. **The visitor startled my brothers. It was unexpected. My brothers were unsuspecting.**

   _____

8. **The squirrel leaped out of the tree house. It was frightened. It was in a big hurry.**

   _____

 Write three short sentences on a sheet of paper about a funny experience. Then try to combine them into one sentence. Which sounds better, one sentence with lots of details or two or three shorter sentences each with one detail? Why?

Scholastic Inc.   Summer Express: Between Grades 4 & 5

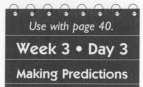
Test Time

➤ **Making predictions** *is using information from a story to determine what will happen next.*

On Monday, Mrs. Bunch announced to her students that they would have their test covering the 50 states and capitals on Friday. In addition to knowing each state's capital, the students would have to be able to fill in all the states' names on a U. S. map. Mrs. Bunch also told the students to be sure to take special notice of their own state. She even put up a poster in front of the classroom showing the state map along with the state motto and flower. Best friends Kevin and Matt both wanted to do well on the test, but each boy studied for the test in a very different way.

Kevin decided to wait until Thursday evening to begin studying. He thought if he learned everything on Thursday, he would be able to remember it better on Friday. After supper on Thursday evening, Kevin took his study notes into the family room so he could watch television while he studied. Mrs. Bunch had given all the students an alphabetical list of the states and their capitals. Kevin read the list over and over again. Then he covered up the capitals and tried to remember what they were as he read each state's name. When he felt that he knew most of the capitals, he then took out his map and began studying where all the states were located. Because Kevin kept taking some time to watch his favorite TV shows, he did not get finished with his studying until very late. The next morning he skipped breakfast so he would not miss his bus and arrive late to school.

Matt, on the other hand, took a different approach to his studying. On Monday evening he made a set of flash cards. On one side of the card, he wrote the name of the state and on the opposite side, he wrote the state's capital. He made one card for each state. He then traced the map of the United States, being careful to outline each state. He took this map to the copy store and made several copies. Now he had some maps on which to practice writing the state names. On Tuesday, Wednesday, and Thursday, Matt spent an hour after supper in his room studying his flash cards and practicing filling in his maps. His mom and dad also helped him by quizzing him about the state capitals while he helped with clearing the table and loading the dishwasher after supper. On his way to school each day, Matt took his flash cards with him on the bus and practiced naming the capitals. Matt went to bed a little earlier on Thursday evening. The next morning he had a good breakfast before catching his bus. On the way to school, he looked over his map and flash cards one last time.

When the boys arrived at school on Friday, they joined their classmates and prepared to take the big test on the states. As Mrs. Bunch handed out the test, Matt noticed that she had taken down the poster of their own state map. Then he received his test and, like his friend Kevin, began to work hard to do his very best.

1. What mistakes do you think Kevin made in the way he studied? _____

_____

_____

_____

2. How was Matt's study plan different from Kevin's? _____

_____

_____

_____

3. The test Mrs. Bunch gave was worth 100 points: one point for naming each state's capital correctly and one point for each state correctly filled in on the map. Write in the number of correct answers you think each boy got on his test.

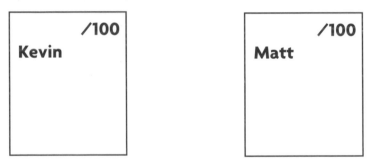

/100

Kevin

/100

Matt

Explain why you think each boy earned the score you wrote. _____

_____

_____

_____

4. Mrs. Bunch included one extra credit question on the test. What do you think it was?

_____

_____

On another sheet of paper, write about a test you thought you were prepared for but it turned out you really were not. Read it to someone in your family.

Scholastic Inc.   Summer Express: Between Grades 4 & 5

Bright Idea!

Each part of a subtraction problem has a name:

$$3,486 \leftarrow \textbf{minuend}$$
$$-\ \ 2,371 \leftarrow \textbf{subtrahend}$$
$$1,115 \leftarrow \textbf{difference}$$

Find each missing subtrahend by subtracting the difference from the minuend.

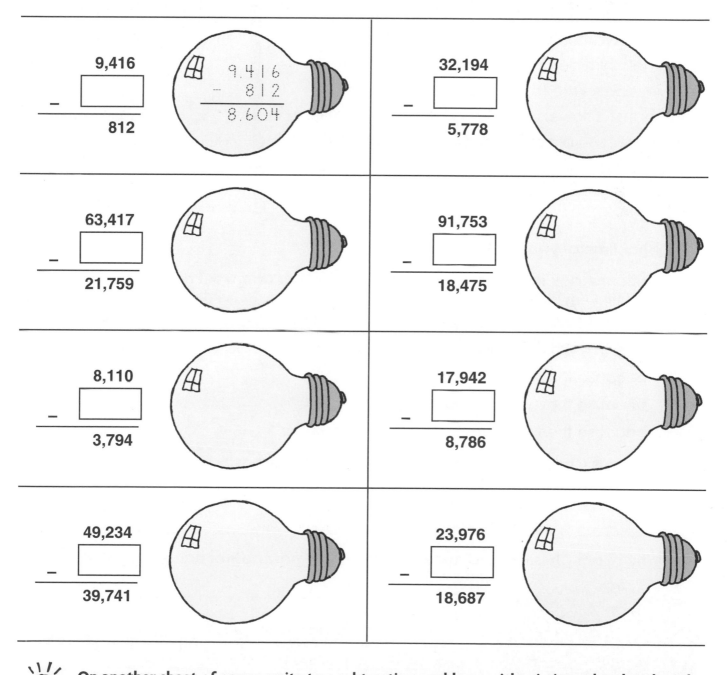

9,416
−
812

9,416
− 812
8,604

32,194
−
5,778

63,417
−
21,759

91,753
−
18,475

8,110
−
3,794

17,942
−
8,786

49,234
−
39,741

23,976
−
18,687

On another sheet of paper, write two subtraction problems with missing subtrahends. Ask someone in your family to help you solve the problems.

Flower Fun

To **draw conclusions** *is to use the information in a story to make a logical assumption.*

Aaaaaahhhhh! It was that time of year again—time to plant flowers. Christina and her dad were trying to decide what kind of flowers to plant this year. Her dad showed her an ad in the morning paper. He wanted Christina to check it out so she could help him determine what they should buy. The two always like to surprise Christina's mom with beautiful flowers before her "big day" in May. Christina was surprised to see Flower Power was having a sale. She knew they had better hurry to the store.

FLOWER POWER SALE
Beautiful flowers of all kinds
— annuals and perennials—
are all on sale — 25% OFF!
All pots and hanging baskets
are on sale, too
Buy one, get one FREE!
Reg. $3.99 to $49.99
Hurry! Sale ends Tuesday!
Flower Power
2418 Harbor Ave.

1. **What time of year is it?** _____

2. **Circle the day in May on which Christina and her dad want her mother to enjoy beautiful flowers.**

   Father's Day   Earth Day   Mother's Day   Easter

3. **Circle why Christina and her dad will probably go to Flower Power today.**

   because they are having a sale

   because they want to plant today

   because the two always plant flowers together

4. **Why was Christina surprised that Flower Power was having a sale?** _____

   _____

   _____

5. **Why might Christina and her dad want to buy new pots or hanging baskets?**

   _____

6. **Why does the ad say to hurry?** _____

   _____

Scholastic Inc.   Summer Express: Between Grades 4 & 5

Behind the Special Effects in Today's Hit Movies

Find and mark the ten grammar errors.

Dear State-of-the-Art,

Recently, I seen the movie *Detonation*, starring Arnold Morphus. It had a lot of great special effect. But, the part I likeded best come near the end. There were not no car chases, and not even any space aliens in the scene. The two characters was just talking. How did they do that?

Signed,

Curious

Dear Curious,

The part of the movie that you liked is called *acting*. Acting requires that the stars act, talk, and make gestures just like real people. Though acting in todays' movies is quite rare, believe it or not, in the olden days, acting was actually quite common in movies!
Signed,

State-of-the-Art

Dear State-of-the-Art,

How did they make the four cockroaches speak its lines in the movie *Roach Motel*?
Signed,

PUZZLED

Dear Puzzled,

This is an easy one! They just hold up cue cards. The roach read their lines right off the cue cards.
Signed,

State-of-the-Art

Show Time

 Sometimes a writer can change the order of the words in a sentence to make it more interesting.

The telephone rang just as the girls were about to leave.
Just as the girls were about to leave, the telephone rang.

Gina decided to answer it in spite of the time.
In spite of the time, Gina decided to answer it.

Do not forget to add a comma when you begin a sentence with a clause or a phrase that cannot stand alone as in the second and last sentences.

Rewrite each sentence by changing the order of the words.

1. **Marta watched for the bus while Gina answered the phone.**

   _____

2. **The caller hung up just as Gina said "Hello."**

   _____

3. **The girls were going to miss the one o'clock show unless they hurried.**

   _____

4. **The bus had already come and gone by the time they got to the corner.**

   _____

5. **The next bus to town finally showed up after the girls had waited a half hour.**

   _____

6. **The girls decided to catch the four o'clock show because they missed the earlier show.**

   _____

7. **They wouldn't have to stand in line later because Gina bought the tickets first.**

   _____

8. **Gina and Marta were at the theater by three o'clock even though it was early.**

   _____

9. **They bought a tub of popcorn and drinks once they were inside.**

   _____

Helping Your Child Get Ready: Week 4

These are the skills your child will be working on this week.

Math
- geometry
- multiplication facts

Reading
- drawing conclusions
- reading for details

Writing
- revising

Vocabulary
- suffixes

Grammar
- parts of speech
- run-on sentences

Here are some activities you and your child might enjoy.

Egg-citing Science Here's a quick and easy science activity. Ask your child if he or she thinks an egg will float in a bowl of water. Have him or her try it. Then add salt, one teaspoon at a time. Does this make a difference? Have him or her do research to find out why.

Zero Is a Hero To help your child understand how important zero is, have him or her look at a few of your grocery store receipts. Whenever a zero appears, have him or her transpose it. For example, .07 would become .70. Have your child add up the new numbers and compare the old and new totals.

Word Sleuths Give your child a newspaper and a highlighter pen. Have him or her search the newspaper trying to find five words he or she doesn't know. Model how to find the meaning of the word (using context clues, the etymology of the word, or the dictionary).

Survey Says . . . What is each family member's favorite treat? Have your child survey the family and share the results.

Your child might enjoy reading the following books:

Trial by Journal
by Kate Klise

Nim's Island
by Wendy Orr

Catwings
by Ursula K. LeGuin

	Cake	Brownies	Cookies	Cupcakes
JOSE	✓			✓
JUAN	✓		✓	✓
CARLOS	✓	✓	✓	✓
ROSA		✓	✓	

's Incentive Chart: Week 4

This week, I plan to read_____ minutes each day.

CHART YOUR PROGRESS HERE.

Week 1	Day 1	Day 2	Day 3	Day 4	Day 5
I read for...	minutes	minutes	minutes	minutes	minutes
Put a sticker to show you completed each day's work.					

Congratulations!

Wow! You did a great job this week!

#1

Place sticker here.

Parent or Caregiver's Signature_____

The State of Apples

A **suffix** is a group of letters that are added to the end of a word and can add meaning to it. Some common suffixes and their meanings are listed in the box.

-ous	full of	**-ward**	direction
-less	without	**-ity**	condition of
-ment	action or process	**-en**	to make
-ent	one who	**-ology**	science or study of
-an	relating to	**-ily**	in what manner

One state grows enough apples for everyone in the world to have 18 pounds of apples a year. Do you know which state this is? To find out, use the suffixes to write a word for each definition. The letters in the boxes will answer the question.

1. **in the direction of the east**   __ __ __ __ ☐ __ __ __

2. **in a hearty manner**   __ __ ☐ __ __ __ __

3. **one who resides in a place**   __ __ ☐ __ __ __ __ __

4. **full of treachery**   __ __ __ __ __ __ ☐ __ __

5. **relating to America**   __ __ __ __ __ ☐ __ __

6. **action of governing**   __ __ __ __ __ __ ☐ __ __ __

7. **the study of animals**   __ __ __ __ __ ☐ __ __

8. **the condition of being necessary**   __ __ __ __ __ __ __ ☐ __

9. **without noise**   __ ☐ __ __ __ __ __ __ __

10. **to make weak**   __ __ __ __ __ ☐

Geometric Terminology

Match the geometric terms on the left side of the page to the correct shape on the right. Use a ruler or a straightedge to draw a line from the term to the shape (dot to dot). Your line will pass through a number and a letter. The number tells you where to write your letter in the code boxes to answer the riddle below.

What should you do if Godzilla suddenly starts to cry?

pentagon •

ray •

    8   **L**

intersecting lines •   **12**   **N**

rectangle •   **3**

           M

line •   **6**   **E**

      A

triangle •   **14**   **N**   **B**

      2

point •   **9**

  10   **D**

perpendicular lines •

    4   **U**

circle •   **7**

          A

line segment • **13**

square •   **5**   **F**

            R

hexagon • **11** **1**   **L** **I**

parallel lines •

octagon •

1	2	3	4		5	6		7	8	9	10	11	12	13	14

A Timely Business

*To **draw conclusions** is to use the information in a story to make a logical assumption.*

April 15, 1860—The mail did get through! The pony express mail delivery service is happy to announce that its riders finished the first complete run from Saint Joseph, Missouri, to Sacramento, California. It originated on April 3.

For those of you unfamiliar with the pony express, this impressive service employs men who ride fast ponies or horses, relay-style, across a 1,966-mile trail. These men carry letters and small packages. They promise delivery from one end of the trail to the other in 10 days or less!

Finally, there is a way to communicate long distance with friends and acquaintances. You will not have to rely on slow boats or stagecoaches. About 180 riders, 400 fast horses, and 190 pony express stations make up the pony express. Its riders are generally of small build, and many are teenagers. A day's work consists of about a 75-mile trip, with stops at several stations. The stations are about 10 to 15 miles apart. Riders earn about $100 to $150 a month.

Currently, it costs $5.00 to send half an ounce of mail. However, the price could fall to $1.00 in the future if the service continues to do well. Mail usually travels at a rate of about 200 miles a day.

The pony express operates both day and night to ensure timely delivery of important letters and packages. Its riders work in all kinds of weather and even face attacks by Indians. Be kind if you see a hard-working rider.

October 26, 1861—Sad news for the pony express. After operating for only about 19 months, the service closed its doors today. This came just 2 days after the opening of the transcontinental telegraph, a device that has revolutionized long-distance communication. Needless to say, the pony express faces huge monetary losses.

The closing comes just months after the pony express service boasted of a 7-day, 17-hour delivery from St. Joseph, Missouri, to Sacramento, California. The record-breaking ride delivered a copy of President Abraham Lincoln's first address to Congress.

1. **Underline each statement that could have happened after the pony express closed.**

   People relied on boats and stagecoaches for mail delivery.

   Pony express riders had to find new jobs.

   There were many fast horses for sale.

   News traveled more quickly by means of the transcontinental telegraph.

2. How do you think people felt about the pony express closing._____

_____

_____

3. Circle how you think the pony express riders felt after the pony express closed.

   relieved   sad   defeated   enlightened

4. Underline what you think would have happened to the pony express if it had stayed
   open after the transcontinental telegraph opened.

   The pony express would have hired more riders.

   People would have stopped using the pony express once they realized how
   much more efficient it was to communicate over distance by means of the
   transcontinental telegraph.

   The pony express would have built several more trails for their riders to use.

5. Find words from the story to match each definition. Then circle each word in the puzzle.
   The words go across, up, down, or backward.

   hires and pays _____

   having a strong impact on _____

   made up of _____

   began _____

   people you know, but not very well _____

   brought about a major change _____

K	A	C	Q	U	A	I	N	T	A	N	C	E	S	C
R	D	L	N	C	T	M	G	O	G	O	Z	R	Y	O
N	E	A	O	M	O	P	N	I	N	E	Y	P	O	N
H	U	C	I	V	E	R	W	Z	U	S	H	S	L	S
O	K	T	Q	N	D	E	I	P	C	O	I	E	P	I
J	S	C	I	U	E	S	M	N	L	P	J	S	M	S
M	A	I	R	E	T	S	F	S	A	I	Y	I	E	T
D	E	Z	I	N	O	I	T	U	L	O	V	E	R	S
D	R	Q	O	O	R	E	V	O	L	U	T	I	O	N
Y	C	U	B	A	D	E	T	A	N	I	G	I	R	O

Railroads were built across the United States in the late 1800s. On another sheet
of paper, write how you think this changed communication in the United States.

50

Scholastic Inc. Summer Express: Between Grades 4 & 5

Two at the Zoo

Don't read this story yet! Give it to a partner and ask him or her to tell you the parts of speech under the blanks below. You give a word for each part of speech, and your partner writes it in the blank. Then he or she writes the words in the story and reads the story aloud.

1. _____
   FRIEND'S NAME

2. _____
   ADJECTIVE

3. _____
   YOUR TOWN

4. _____
   FRIEND'S NAME

5. _____
   NOUN

6. _____
   ANIMAL

7. _____
   ADJECTIVE

8. _____
   NOUN

9. _____
   VERB

10. _____
    NOUN

11. _____
    ADJECTIVE

12. _____
    FRIEND'S NAME

13. _____
    ADJECTIVE

14. _____
    VERB

15. _____
    NOUN

The whole thing was an accident. My friend

_____ and I just wanted to spend a
         1

_____ day at the _____ Zoo.
         2   3

Who knew that _____ would slip
                          4

on a _____ and bump into the
                5

_____ cage? The door sprang open, and
         6

the _____ creature inside, which was
           7

eating a _____, ran out of the cage. It
                  8

went nuts! I've never seen an animal _____
                                                      9

like that before! The zookeeper came out with a giant

_____ to catch the _____
         10   11

beast. The zookeeper's eyesight wasn't good. He

caught _____ instead. Don't worry—
              12

my friend now lives in a _____ cage and
                                    13

can _____ all day long, or even play with
           14

a _____ .
        15

Keeps On Going

*Writers sometimes make the mistake of running together two or more sentences without telling how the ideas are related. This kind of sentence is called a **run-on sentence**.*

Kansas holds the record for having the largest ball of twine in the United States can you believe it weighs over 17,000 pounds in fact, the giant ball is 40 feet in circumference, 11 feet tall, and made up of more than 1,100 miles of twine!

To fix a run-on sentence, identify each complete thought or idea and break it into shorter sentences.

Kansas holds the record for having the largest ball of twine in the United States. Can you believe it weighs over 17,000 pounds? In fact, the giant ball is 40 feet in circumference, 11 feet tall, and made up of more than 1,100 miles of twine!

Rewrite each run-on sentence correctly. Remember to begin and end each sentence correctly.

1. **Did you know that the United States is the top meat-eating country in the world each person consumes about 260 pounds of meat each year beef is the most commonly eaten meat.**

   _____

   _____

   _____

2. **Have you ever noticed that Abraham Lincoln faces right on a penny he is the only president on a U.S. coin who does Sacagawea faces right on the new dollar coin, but she was not a president?**

   _____

   _____

   _____

3. **It would be fantastic to have a robot to do all my chores, help do my homework, and play games I really think the day will come unfortunately, it won't come soon enough for me.**

   _____

   _____

   _____

Scholastic Inc.   Summer Express: Between Grades 4 & 5

Under the Big Top

 *The answer to a multiplication problem is called the **product**.*
*The numbers being multiplied are called **factors**.*

Multiply. Then use each product and the code to answer the riddles.

What happened to the human cannonball at the circus?

___	___		___	___	___		___	___	___	___	___
4 x 6	6 x 3		7 x 7	3 x 4	8 x 8		8 x 3	6 x 8	7 x 9	2 x 9	8 x 7

___	___	___		___	___	___	___	___		___	___
6 x 2	8 x 9	7 x 8		9 x 9	8 x 6	9 x 7	3 x 6	7 x 8		7 x 6	9 x 8

___	___	___		___	___	___	___		___	___	___ !
5 x 9	6 x 4	9 x 2		8 x 8	4 x 3	6 x 6	6 x 3		8 x 7	2 x 6	5 x 5

What happened to the kid who ran away with the circus?

___	___		___	___	___
3 x 8	2 x 9		4 x 6	3 x 4	8 x 7

___	___		___	___	___	___	___
9 x 5	6 x 7		9 x 3	7 x 9	8 x 6	9 x 8	5 x 8

___	___		___	___	___	___ !
6 x 8	5 x 9		3 x 9	2 x 6	5 x 3	9 x 6

A = 12	H = 24	O = 42	V = 21
B = 27	I = 48	P = 16	W = 49
C = 15	J = 4	Q = 28	X = 1
D = 56	K = 54	R = 63	Y = 25
E = 18	L = 8	S = 64	Z = 2
F = 81	M = 36	T = 45	
G = 40	N = 72	U = 0	

Week 4 • Day 4

A Long School Year

 Have you ever accidentally left out words when you write? Whenever you write, it is always a good idea to proofread for words that may be missing. Here is an example of what to do when you want to add a missing word as you proofread.

           e-mail
I got an ∧ from my friend last night.

    met
We ∧ last summer when my family was in Japan.

Read the passage below about school in Japan. Twenty-one words are missing. Figure out what they are and add them to the sentences. Use the ∧ symbol to show where each missing word belongs. Then write each missing word above the sentence. Hint: Every sentence has at least one missing word.

     How would like to go to school on Saturdays? If you lived in the of Japan,

that's just where you'd be each Saturday morning. I have a who lives in Japan.

Yuichi explained that attend classes five and one-half a week. The day is on

Saturday. I was also surprised to that the Japanese school is one of the longest

in the world—over 240 days. It begins in the of April. While we have over two

months off each, students in Japan get their in late July and August. School

then again in fall and ends in March. The people of believe that a good is very

important. Children are required to attend school from the age of six to the of

fifteen. They have elementary and middle just like we do. Then most go on to

school for another three years. Yuichi says that students work very because the

standards are so high. He and some of his friends even extra classes after

school. They all want to get into a good someday.

 Write several sentences on a sheet of paper about something that interests you. Rewrite the sentences on another sheet of paper, this time leaving out a key word in each one. Challenge someone at home to add the missing words. Then compare the two sets of sentences.

Amazing Animals

All animals are fascinating, and some are truly amazing! For example, did you know that sharks' teeth are as hard as steel, or that kangaroo rats can survive longer without water than camels? Study the chart below to learn more about several amazing animals.

Animal	Where It Lives	Vertebrate or Invertebrate	Fascinating Fact
albatross	near most oceans	vertebrate	can sleep while flying
caterpillar	all over the world	invertebrate	has three times as many muscles as humans
chameleon	forests in Africa and Madagascar	vertebrate	can move its eyes in two different directions at the same time
cockroach	all over the world	invertebrate	can live for up to a week without a head
crocodile	tropical climates	vertebrate	eats only about 50 meals a year
giant squid	oceans throughout the world	invertebrate	has eyes bigger than a human head
giraffe	grasslands in Africa	vertebrate	is the tallest of animals; has only seven neck bones
penguin	in the southern half of the world with cold ocean waters	vertebrate	has eggs kept warm by male until hatched
octopus	oceans throughout the world	invertebrate	has three hearts
shark	oceans throughout the world	vertebrate	never runs out of teeth
snail	almost everywhere—forests, deserts, rivers, ponds, oceans	invertebrate	can sleep for almost three years without waking up
sperm whale	oceans throughout the world	vertebrate	can hold its breath for up to 60 minutes

1. Which animal(s) live in the ocean? _____

_____

2. What do the giant squid and the chameleon have in common? _____

_____

3. Which animal would delight the "Tooth Fairy"? _____

4. Label the animals below with a *V* if they have backbones. _____

_____

5. Which animals live all, or nearly all, over the world? _____

_____

6. Which animal is very muscular? _____

7. Which animal eats an average of about once a week? _____

8. Which animal can live headless for about a week? _____

9. What is fascinating about a chameleon's eyes? _____

_____

10. Which animal is a "super snoozer"? _____

11. Which animal can hold its breath for nearly an hour? _____

12. Which animal has seven bones in its neck? _____

Read about another animal. Find a fascinating fact about it to share with someone in your family.

Helping Your Child Get Ready: Week 5

These are the skills your child will be working on this week.

Math
- multiplication with regrouping
- area and perimeter

Reading
- summarizing
- comparing and contrasting

Writing
- parts of a paragraph
- topic sentences

Vocabulary
- word roots

Grammar
- subject-verb agreement

Here are some activities you and your child might enjoy.

Double Meanings Have your child figure out the two (or more!) meanings for each of these words: *bob, hamper, maroon, fair.* Think of more double-meaning words to challenge your child.

Penny Flick In this measuring skill-building game, competitors flick a penny across the floor or table top. The winner is the one whose coin comes to rest closest to 1 meter from the starting line.

Root-Word Hunting Ask your child to think of as many words as possible that have the root word *aqua.* Then have him or her figure out the meaning of this root. Try this with other roots like *graph, spect,* and *geo.*

Memorize a Poem Encourage your child to memorize a short poem. Have him or her read the poem repeatedly (a great way to build reading fluency). Suggest that he or she learn one line a day. Agree on a special treat when he or she has successfully memorized the poem.

Your child might enjoy reading the following books:

King of Shadows
by Susan Cooper

Ella Enchanted
by Gail Carson Levine

A Year Down Yonder
by Richard Peck

_____'s Incentive Chart: Week 5
Name Here

This week, I plan to read_____ minutes each day.

CHART YOUR PROGRESS HERE.

Week 1	Day 1	Day 2	Day 3	Day 4	Day 5
I read for...	minutes	minutes	minutes	minutes	minutes
Put a sticker to show you completed each day's work.					

Congratulations!

Wow! You did a great job this week!

#1

Place sticker here.

Parent or Caregiver's Signature_____

The Root of the Matter

*A word can have parts. The main part of a word, or **root**, contains the basic meaning. Here are some common roots.*

> **spec, vid, vis, scop** = see
>
> **aud** = hear
>
> **phon, son** = sound
>
> **tact** = touch
>
> **clam, claim** = shout
>
> **dic** = speak

The root is missing from one word in each sentence. Use context clues and the meaning of the roots to complete each word with its root.

1. **My grandfather listens to his old 45s on a _____ograph.**

2. **NASA lost con_____ with the astronauts during reentry.**

3. **The _____or of the crowd was almost deafening.**

4. **We heard a piano _____ata by Beethoven at the concert.**

5. **Everyone in the _____ience seemed to enjoy the play.**

6. **Hometown _____tators cheered as their team ran onto the field.**

7. **The crack in the plate is barely _____ible.**

8. **Why don't you come over and watch a _____eo with us?**

9. **The suspect pro_____ed that he was not guilty of the charges.**

10. **The students used a micro_____e to study the plant cells.**

11. **I will _____tate the list of words so listen carefully.**

On another sheet of paper, list the words you made. Define each one in your own words. Then use a dictionary to check your definitions. Make corrections if needed.

Here are some more common roots. Find out what each root means. Knowing these roots will help you figure out the meaning of unfamiliar words.

act	aero	aqua	bio	cycl	fac	form	geo	gram
liber	loc	mar	mob	nat	pod	photo	ques	san
saur	scribe	sign	terr	therm	trib	voc	void	volv

Subject-Verb Agreement

The **subject** and **verb** in a sentence must agree in person (first, second, or third) and in number. A singular subject takes a singular verb, and a plural subject takes a plural verb.

A. **Draw one line under the subject in each sentence. Draw two lines under the verb. Then write *S* if the subject and verb are singular or *P* if they are plural.**

1. A conductor beats time with a baton. _____

2. Many musicians memorize their music. _____

3. The principal violinist leads the other musicians. _____

4. The concert hall buzzes with voices. _____

5. Mariachi bands consist of violins, guitars, trumpets, and singers. _____

6. The singers and lead guitarist often practice together. _____

7. Jazz groups perform at the State Theater in our city. _____

8. A pianist works hard to prepare for a performance. _____

A. **Write the present tense form of the verb in parentheses ( ) that correctly completes each sentence.**

1. Mariachi bands _____ all over the world. (play)

2. My cousin _____ everywhere with the band. (go)

3. The trumpet player always _____ a radio with him. (take)

4. The guitarist in this band also _____ music. (write)

5. The drummer _____ the conductor carefully. (watch)

6. My favorite singer _____ two songs on the Top Ten list. (have)

7. My brother and I _____ to them every morning. (listen)

8. Jamal and Denise _____ the city every year. (visit)

Scholastic Inc. Summer Express: Between Grades 4 & 5

The Faraway Country

To multiply with a 2-digit factor that requires regrouping, follow these steps.

1. Multiply the ones.
   Regroup if needed.
   7 x 3 = 21

2. Multiply the bottom factor in the ones column with
   the top factor in the tens column. Add the extra tens.
   6 x 3 = 18   18 + 2 = 20

$$\begin{array}{r} 2 \\ 6\,7 \\ x\quad 3 \\ \hline 1 \end{array}$$

$$\begin{array}{r} 2 \\ 6\,7 \\ x\quad 3 \\ \hline 2\,0\,1 \end{array}$$

Multiply.

A.

$$\begin{array}{r} 48 \\ x\quad 3 \\ \hline \end{array}$$
$$\begin{array}{r} 24 \\ x\quad 7 \\ \hline \end{array}$$
$$\begin{array}{r} 73 \\ x\quad 4 \\ \hline \end{array}$$

B.

$$\begin{array}{r} 57 \\ x\quad 7 \\ \hline \end{array}$$
$$\begin{array}{r} 63 \\ x\quad 9 \\ \hline \end{array}$$
$$\begin{array}{r} 56 \\ x\quad 3 \\ \hline \end{array}$$

C.

$$\begin{array}{r} 98 \\ x\quad 2 \\ \hline \end{array}$$
$$\begin{array}{r} 64 \\ x\quad 8 \\ \hline \end{array}$$
$$\begin{array}{r} 57 \\ x\quad 8 \\ \hline \end{array}$$
$$\begin{array}{r} 35 \\ x\quad 9 \\ \hline \end{array}$$
$$\begin{array}{r} 23 \\ x\quad 8 \\ \hline \end{array}$$
$$\begin{array}{r} 82 \\ x\quad 6 \\ \hline \end{array}$$

D.

$$\begin{array}{r} 95 \\ x\quad 9 \\ \hline \end{array}$$
$$\begin{array}{r} 77 \\ x\quad 6 \\ \hline \end{array}$$
$$\begin{array}{r} 83 \\ x\quad 9 \\ \hline \end{array}$$
$$\begin{array}{r} 96 \\ x\quad 8 \\ \hline \end{array}$$
$$\begin{array}{r} 28 \\ x\quad 4 \\ \hline \end{array}$$
$$\begin{array}{r} 96 \\ x\quad 5 \\ \hline \end{array}$$

Switzerland is famous for the magnificent Swiss Alps. Waterfalls are formed by many of the mountain streams. The highest waterfall is Giessbach Falls. To find out how many meters high this waterfall is, add the products in Row A.

What's the Topic?

Every paragraph has a topic sentence that tells the main idea of the paragraph, or what it is about. It usually answers several of these questions:

Who?   What?   Where?   When?   Why?   How?

Here are some examples.

The doe and her fawn faced many dangers in the forest.
We were amazed by our guest's rude behavior.
Baking bread from scratch is really not so difficult, or so I thought.
Getting up in the morning is the hardest thing to do.

Did these topic sentences grab your attention? A good topic sentence should.

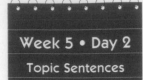

Here are some topics. Write a topic sentence for each one.

1. **convincing someone to try octopus soup**

   _____

2. **an important person in your life**

   _____

3. **an embarrassing moment**

   _____

4. **the importance of Independence Day**

   _____

   _____

5. **lunchtime at the school cafeteria**

   _____

Now list some topics of your own. Then write a topic sentence for each one.

_____
Topic #1

_____   _____
Topic #2   **Topic #3**

_____
Topic sentence #1

_____
Topic sentence #2

_____
Topic sentence #3

Scholastic Inc.   *Summer Express: Between Grades 4 & 5*

Parts of a Paragraph

A **paragraph** is a group of sentences that tells about one main idea. The **topic sentence** tells the main idea and is usually the first sentence. **Supporting sentences** tell more about the main idea. The **closing sentence** of a paragraph often retells the main idea in a different way. Here are the parts for one paragraph.

Paragraph Title: **Starting Over**

Topic Sentence: **Today started off badly and only got worse.**

Supporting Sentences: 1. **Everyone in my family woke up late this morning.**

2. **I had only 15 minutes to get ready and catch the bus.**

3. **I dressed as fast as I could, grabbed an apple and my backpack, and raced to get to the bus stop on time.**

4. **Fortunately, I just made it.**

5. **Unfortunately, the bus was pulling away when several kids pointed out that I had on two different shoes.**

Closing Sentence: **At that moment, I wanted to start the day over.**

When you write a paragraph, remember these rules:

• **Indent** the first line to let readers know that you are beginning a paragraph.
• **Capitalize** the first word of each sentence.
• **Punctuate** each sentence correctly (? ! . ,).

Use all the information above to write the paragraph. Be sure to follow the rules.

_____
paragraph title

_____

_____

_____

_____

_____

_____

_____

Math's Got It Covered

This soccer player sure has a lot of ground to cover. Just how much exactly?
Look at the picture and answer the questions.

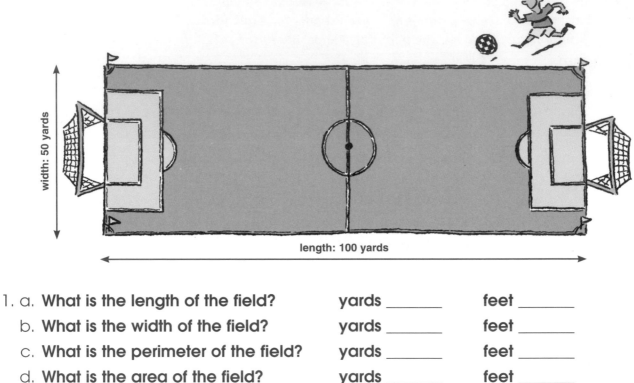

width: 50 yards

length: 100 yards

1. a. **What is the length of the field?**   yards _____   feet _____
   b. **What is the width of the field?**   yards _____   feet _____
   c. **What is the perimeter of the field?**   yards _____   feet _____
   d. **What is the area of the field?**   yards _____   feet _____

2. a. **What is the perimeter of half of the field?**   yards _____   feet _____
   b. **What is the area of half of the field?**   yards _____   feet _____

3. **Imagine a field with a length of 130 yards and a width of 75 yards.**
   a. **What is the perimeter of that field?** _____
   b. **What is the area of that field?** _____

All-Star Math!

Is the perimeter of half the field what
you expected? Why or why not?

_____

_____

length: 1 unit

length: 1 unit

area = 1 square
unit
perimeter = 4 units

area = length x width
perimeter = sum of the sides

64

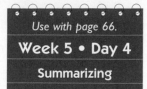
The Wonderful Whale

 A **summary** tells the most important parts of a story.

For each paragraph, circle the sentence that tells the most important part.

1.   The largest animal that has ever lived is the blue whale. It can grow up to 300 feet long and weigh more than 100 tons. Whales, for the most part, are enormous creatures. However, some kinds only grow to be 10 to 15 feet long.

The blue whale is the largest animal.
Most whales are enormous creatures.
Some whales are only 10 to 15 feet long.

2.   Whales look a lot like fish. However, whales differ from fish in many ways. For example, the tail fin of a fish is up and down; the tail fin of a whale is sideways. Fish breathe through gills. Whales have lungs and must come to the surface from time to time to breathe. Whales can hold their breath for a very long time. The sperm whale can hold its breath for about an hour.

Whales and fish do not share similar breathing patterns.
Whales can hold their breath for about an hour.
Whales might look a lot like fish, but the two are very different.

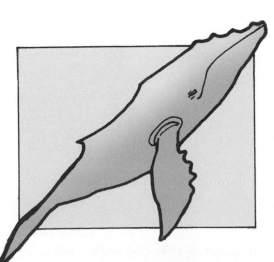

3.   Baleen whales have no teeth. Toothed whales have teeth. Baleen whales have hundreds of thin plates in their mouth. They use these plates to strain out food from the water. Their diet consists of tiny plants and animals. Toothed whales eat such foods as other fish, cuttlefish, and squid.

Whales can be divided into two groups—baleen and toothed.
Baleen whales have plates in their mouths; toothed whales do not.
Toothed whales use their teeth to chew their food.

4. Whales have a layer of fat called blubber. Blubber keeps them warm. Whales can live off their blubber for a long time if food is scarce. Blubber also helps whales float, as it is lighter than water.

   Layers of fat are called blubber.
   Blubber is very important to whales and has many purposes.
   Blubber is what makes whales float.

5. **Write the main idea of each paragraph to complete a summary about whales.**

   _____

   _____

   _____

   _____

6. **Fill in the whale and the fish with the following descriptions. Write the descriptions that are specific to each on the spaces that don't overlap. Write what the two have in common in the shared space.**

   can hold breath for long time   people love to watch

   gills   tail fin sideways

   live in ponds   tail fin up and down

   live in oceans   lungs

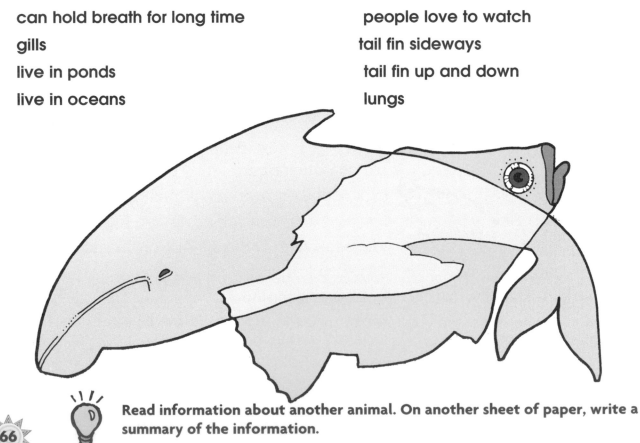

   Read information about another animal. On another sheet of paper, write a summary of the information.

A Difficult Choice

Emily and Zach are confused! Their parents told them they could choose between Massachusetts and Arizona for their vacation this summer, and they think both states seem pretty awesome. Emily has always wanted to visit Boston, the capital of Massachusetts. Zach and she both agree that strolling along the Freedom Trail would be pretty neat. Walking the trail would enable them to see Boston's most famous historic landmarks, like the site of the school Ben Franklin attended and the Old State House. It was built in 1713 and served as the seat of the colonial government.

Emily and Zach both love the beach. If they went to Massachusetts, they could spend a few days at the beaches on Cape Cod. Emily loves boogie boarding, and Zach is great at body surfing. They both enjoy building sandcastles with their mom and dad.

Zach finds learning about Native Americans fascinating and has always wanted to travel along the Apache Trail in Arizona. This mountain highway passes Native American ruins in Tonto National Forest. Emily is not as interested in traveling along this trail as Zach, but they both would like to visit Phoenix, the capital, and then travel to Grand Canyon National Park and Meteor Crater. Zach learned in science class that Meteor Crater is a hole over 4,000 feet wide and 520 feet deep that was created when a huge object from space fell to Earth. The object went so deep that it has never been found. Zach would really like to try to locate it. Emily thinks he is crazy! If experienced scientists and researchers cannot find it, Zach might as well not even bother to try.

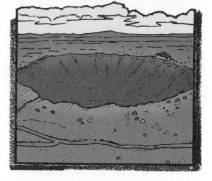

If Arizona is the chosen state, Emily and Zach would also like to stop at a few other places. Arizona is home to fifteen national monuments. That is more than any other state.

The only drawback for Zach if they choose Arizona would be the heat. It is very hot and dry in this southwestern state. Arizona has a lot of what Massachusetts does not— desert land. Once in July in Arizona, it got up to 127°F !

Massachusetts, on the other hand, is located in the northeastern United States. Here, Zach and Emily and their parents could enjoy mild temperatures of about 75° F. Their parents love hot weather, but Zach and Emily do not really like to sweat. Therefore, both know that they would prefer the climate of Massachusetts.

How will they ever decide to which state they should travel? If only they could take two trips!

1. "Pack" each suitcase to describe the two regions.

   Tonto National Forest

   Old State House

   Freedom Trail

   mild climate

   Phoenix

   Boston

   very hot

   Cape Cod

   Apache Trail

   Grand Canyon

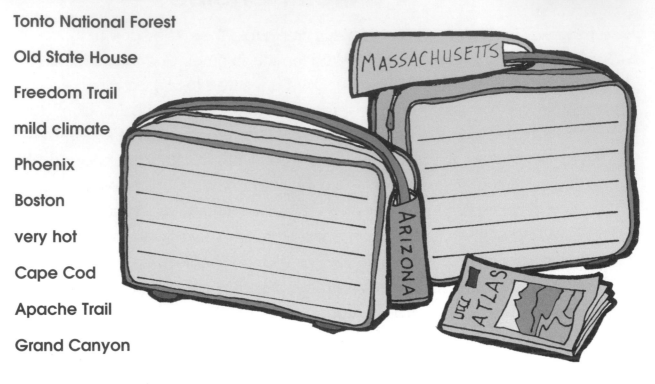

2. Circle things both Emily and Zach like or would like to see.

building sandcastles	Apache Trail	hot weather	beach
Meteor Crater	surfboarding	Freedom Trail	sweating

3. Write one way Zach and Emily are different from their parents. _____

   _____

4. Write one way the Freedom Trail and the Apache Trail are different. _____

   _____

   _____

5. How do Zach and Emily spend their time differently at the beach? _____

   _____

6. How are Zach and Emily's feelings different when it comes to finding the missing object at Meteor Crater? _____

   _____

Read about a state you would like to visit. On another sheet of paper, write five differences between the state you chose and the state in which you live.

Scholastic Inc.   Summer Express: Between Grades 4 & 5

Helping Your Child Get Ready: Week 6

These are the skills your child will be working on this week.

Math
- subtracting fractions
- adding money

Reading
- making inferences
- comparing and contrasting

Writing
- writing topic sentences

Vocabulary
- homophones

Spelling
- spelling patterns

Here are some activities you and your child might enjoy.

Compound It Ask your child to list as many compound words as possible that contain the word *house*.

Compliment Jar Create a compliment jar. Label a clear plastic jar with the word "Compliments." Invite everyone in your home to write a compliment for another family member on a slip of paper and place it in the jar. Once a week, invite your child to read the compliments aloud to the rest of the family.

Circle Graph Have your child make a circle graph showing how he or she spends time in a typical 24-hour period.

Window Poem Have your child write a window poem. Have him or her look out a window and write a short poem about what he or she sees.

Your child might enjoy reading the following books:

The Man in the Ceiling
by Jules Feiffer

The Facts and Fictions of Minna Pratt
by Patricia MacLachlan

Phoebe the Spy
by Judith Berry Griffin

_____
Name Here

's Incentive Chart: Week 6

This week, I plan to read _____ minutes each day.

CHART YOUR PROGRESS HERE.

Week 1	Day 1	Day 2	Day 3	Day 4	Day 5
I read for...	minutes	minutes	minutes	minutes	minutes
Put a sticker to show you completed each day's work.					

Congratulations!

Wow! You did a great job this week!

#1

Place sticker here.

Parent or Caregiver's Signature _____

A Beastly Puzzle

How many three- and four-letter animal names can you find in this puzzle? Words can be spelled by moving from letter to letter along the lines connecting the circles. For example, you can form the word DOG by starting at the D, moving left to the O and then up to the G. There are six more animals names in the puzzle.

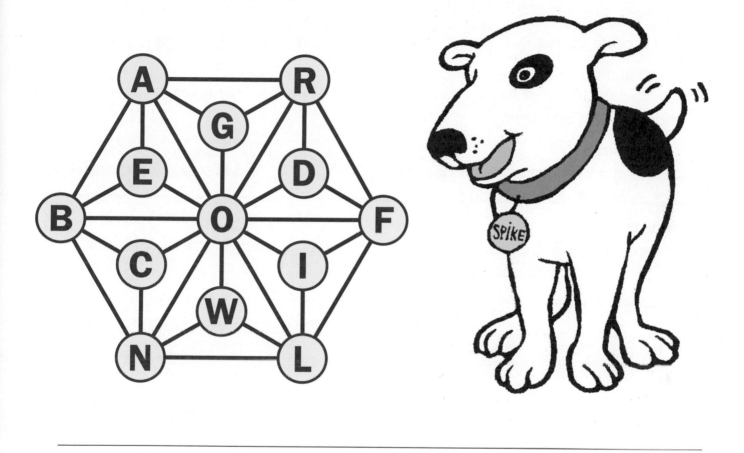

_____

_____

_____

_____

_____

_____

Bonus: There are lots of other words in this puzzle that aren't names of animals. Find as many as you can.

Which One Do You Mean?

 A **homophone** *is a word that sounds just like another word, but it has a different spelling and a different meaning.*

Write the correct homophone in each blank to complete the sentence. Use a dictionary if necessary.

1. **ball, bawl**
   The toddler started to _____ when the dog ran off with her _____.

2. **manner, manor**
   The lord and lady of the _____ displayed a kindly _____ toward their servants and staff.

3. **chute, shoot**
   Just as the cameraman was about to _____ the scene, the actor lost his balance and slid down the _____.

4. **straight, strait**
   The captain skillfully sailed the ship _____ through the treacherous _____ without any difficulty.

5. **weather, whether**
   _____ or not we hold the family reunion outdoors depends completely on the _____ that day.

6. **least, leased**
   According to our neighbors, Mr. Jenkins _____ the house across the street for at _____ two years.

The homophones are used incorrectly in the sentences below. Cross out each incorrect word. On another sheet of paper, rewrite the sentences with the correct words.

7. **I slipped the bridal over my hoarse's head, took the reign, and lead the animal toward the riding path.**

8. **The air to the thrown proved to be a fare ruler.**

9. **Theirs an extra hangar in the close closet.**

10. **We ordered stake sandwiches on toasted hole wheat bred.**

11. **The boys leaped over the creak and duct behind a bolder, hoping they wood not be scene.**

12. **We needed the doe, aloud it to rise, and baked it for an our and a half.**

Topic Talk

Most paragraphs begin with a topic sentence, but it can appear elsewhere in a paragraph. Sometimes a topic sentence is located at the end of a paragraph or even in the middle.

A boiling mass of clouds was almost overhead. A bolt of lightning streaked across the darkened sky. Thunder boomed, and it began to rain and hail. <u>We had to find a safe place quickly!</u> There wasn't a moment to spare because early summer storms sometimes turn into tornadoes.

Read the paragraph again. This time try the topic sentence elsewhere in the paragraph.

Read each paragraph. Notice that each one is missing a topic sentence. Think about the supporting sentences. What main idea do you think they support? Write a topic sentence to tell the main idea of each paragraph. Remember that a topic sentence is not always the first sentence of a paragraph.

1. **The days are growing longer. The winter snows are melting as the temperatures rise. Colorful crocuses are popping up here and there. Robins have begun to return north, and creatures are beginning to come out of their winter burrows.** _____

_____

2. _____

It was fun and easy. Students, parents, and teachers began saving the box tops from all Healthful Foods products. After we collected 100,000 box tops, we mailed them to Healthful Foods headquarters. We earned 10 cents for each box top for a total of $10,000. Our school will use the money to buy computers.

3. **The last weekend in June is quickly approaching. You know what that means.**

_____

This year the festivities will begin at 10:00 A.M. at Twin Lakes Picnic Grove, pavilion 12. As always, there will be music, dancing, lots of great food, games, and some new surprises! We look forward to seeing you.

Fraction Subtraction

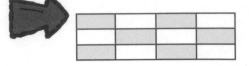

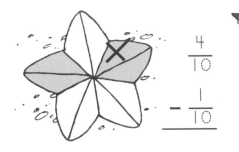

How many squares are there in all? **12**

What fraction of squares are colored? $\frac{6}{12}$

Subtract the fraction of marked-out squares. $\frac{6}{12} - \frac{3}{12} = \frac{3}{12}$

What fraction of colored squares remain unmarked? $\frac{3}{12} = \frac{1}{4}$

Write out the fraction subtraction problem. Subtract. Reduce to lowest terms.

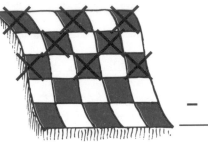

$$\frac{4}{10}$$
$$-\frac{1}{10}$$

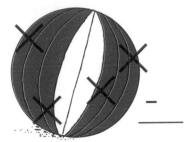

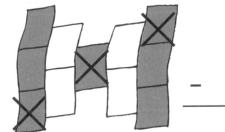

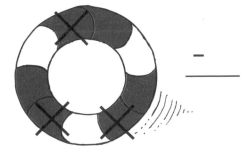

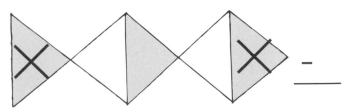

Jason is traveling to the beach with his grandparents. Jason's grandfather told Jason that when they had traveled 5/8 of the way, they would stop to stretch and get a snack. They have only traveled 3/8 of the way. What fraction of the way must Jason wait before they stop?

74

Scholastic Inc.   Summer Express: Between Grades 4 & 5

A Lot of Details

When you are ready to write a topic sentence, think about the main topic or idea of the paragraph you will be writing and the details you plan to include. Then jot down several possible sentences and choose the best one. Remember that a topic sentence can answer several questions: Who? What? Where? When? Why? How?

Tony Hawk
– skateboarder
– in his forties
– turned professional at age 14
– has won more skateboarding contests than anyone
– made history at Summer X Games in 1999—landed a "900"
  (a complete somersault done 2 ½ times in midair)

Possible topic sentences: **There is no other skateboarder like Tony Hawk.**
Tony Hawk is an extraordinary skateboarder.
Tony Hawk is the "old man" of skateboarding.

Here are some topics with details. Write two topic sentences for each one on the lines below.

1. **Pet Rocks**	2. **Komodo Dragon**	3. **A Great Dessert**
— fad in the 1970s — idea came from Gary Dahl, a salesman — sold rocks as pets — came with a manual — manual had tips on how to teach a pet rock tricks	— member of monitor family — grows to 10 feet and weighs 300 pounds — meat eater — dangerous to humans — largest lizard in the world — long neck and tail, strong legs — found on Komodo Island	— slice a banana — add vanilla ice cream — sprinkle on some walnuts — cover with lots of hot fudge sauce — top with mounds of whipped cream and a cherry

1. _____

_____

2. _____

_____

3. _____

_____

Remember that the supporting sentences you write support or tell more about the main idea in your topic sentence. Read the paragraph below. Draw one line under the topic sentence. Draw two lines under the supporting sentences. Check (√) the closing sentence.

Tony Hawk

Tony Hawk is an extraordinary skateboarder. He turned professional when he was only 14 years old. Now in his forties, Tony has won more skateboarding contests than anyone else has. He even made history in 1999 by landing a trick called the "900" at the Summer X Games. Tony Hawk may just be the greatest skateboarder in the world.

Now, review the topics on page 75. Choose one. Then review the details listed about the topic in the box. Next, use the information to write at least three supporting sentences to support the topic sentence you wrote. Include a closing sentence and a title. Write the paragraph below.

_____

_____

_____

_____

_____

_____

_____

Make a list of topics you would like to write about. Choose one. Then list on a sheet of paper details you know about the topic. Do some research if necessary. Then write a topic sentence and several supporting sentences.

Guess the State

Spencer, Jack, Grant, and Kara are new in Mrs. Steen's fifth-grade class. Each of these students came from one of the following states: Pennsylvania, Arizona, Washington, and Massachusetts. They are taking turns giving the class clues about the state from which they moved. The other children are trying to guess the state from the clues.

Use the following clues to help you determine which state was the home of each new student. Write each new student's name on the correct state outline below. Label the state in which all the students now live.

1. Spencer is not from the Keystone State.

2. Grant is not from the south or the east.

3. Kara is not from the south or the west.

4. Jack is not from the south or the west.

5. Grant and Spencer are both from states that border another country.

6. Jack and Kara lived the closest to each other before they moved.

7. Grant used to be able to visit the Space Needle.

8. Many of Spencer's old friends speak Spanish very well.

9. Kara used to live in "the birthplace of the United States."

10. Jack used to vacation on Cape Cod. He also loved strolling along the Freedom Trail.

11. All four children love their new state. It is located in the northeastern corner of the United States. It is the largest New England state. Its nickname is the Pine Tree State. Canada forms its northern boundary.

Greedy Gretchen

Gold! Gold! Gold! Help Greedy Gretchen find the path through Nottingham Forest from her house to the bank. On which path can she collect the most gold? Draw a line to show that path. On another sheet of paper, explain your answer.

Scholastic Inc.   Summer Express: Between Grades 4 & 5

Many Thanks

Giving thanks is a custom among people all around the world. Like the American Thanksgiving, many celebrations began as a way of showing gratitude for a good harvest. In Korea, people have celebrated a fall holiday called Ch'usok for more than 1,000 years. Families prepare special foods using newly harvested crops. On the holiday itself, Koreans give thanks and remember their ancestors. Later in the day, they enjoy a feast of rice cakes, fresh fruit, and vegetable soup. In the United States, Thanksgiving honors a tradition that began in 1621 with the Pilgrims and the Wampanoag Indians. A typical American Thanksgiving includes foods such as turkey, potatoes, cranberries, stuffing, vegetables, and pumpkin pie. Families and friends give thanks not only for their meal, but also for the freedoms they enjoy as Americans.

Write three headings on the diagram. Under each heading, add facts from the passage.

MORE! Find out who Sarah Josepha Hall was and why she is known in the U.S. as "the mother of Thanksgiving."

Testing It Out

Use after completing Many Thanks on page 79.

Fill in the circle of the best answer.

1. **The passage compares—**
   - Ⓐ Americans and Pilgrims
   - Ⓑ kinds of memorial services
   - Ⓒ Ch'usok and Thanksgiving
   - Ⓓ Wampanoags and Koreans

2. **On both holidays, people—**
   - Ⓐ give gifts
   - Ⓑ make rice cakes
   - Ⓒ roast turkeys
   - Ⓓ show gratitude

3. **Both holidays are celebrated—**
   - Ⓐ in the spring
   - Ⓑ before the harvest
   - Ⓒ in the fall
   - Ⓓ around the world

4. **The Korean holiday—**
   - Ⓐ is about the freedoms of Korea
   - Ⓑ is also about ancestor worship
   - Ⓒ began in 1621
   - Ⓓ is more recent than the American holiday

5. **A traditional food on Thanksgiving in the U.S. is—**
   - Ⓐ rice cakes
   - Ⓑ cranberries
   - Ⓒ fresh fruit
   - Ⓓ hot soup

6. **A food that people do not usually eat on Ch'usok is—**
   - Ⓐ fruit
   - Ⓑ vegetables
   - Ⓒ rice
   - Ⓓ turkey

7. **The people celebrating together at both holidays are usually—**
   - Ⓐ family members
   - Ⓑ Americans
   - Ⓒ Pilgrims
   - Ⓓ Koreans

8. **From this passage you can guess that—**
   - Ⓐ Koreans do not eat dessert
   - Ⓑ rice is an important food in Korea
   - Ⓒ all Thanksgivings are the same
   - Ⓓ Americans do not eat rice

Scholastic Inc. *Summer Express: Between Grades 4 & 5*

These are the skills your child will be working on this week.

Math
- measurement
- multiplication word problems
- bar graphs

Reading
- finding the main idea

Writing
- supporting details
- writing a poem
- writing a comparison paragraph

Vocabulary
- analogies

Grammar
- complete sentences

Here are some activities you and your child might enjoy.

Idiom Pictionary Play idiom pictionary. Have your child choose an idiom, such as "apple of my eye" or "turn over a new leaf" and draw a picture of it for others to guess.

Timeline Have your child create a timeline of his or her life. The timeline can start with his or her birth, and include other significant dates such as births of siblings, first tooth, and first day of school.

Comparison Shopping Collect flyers or newspaper ads from several grocery stores. Give your child a list of items you regularly shop for. Have him or her use the flyers and ads to determine which store has the best deals.

Plan the Menu Have your child plan your dinner menu and then help cook the meal. Ask him or her to be sure to think about the food pyramid nutritional guidelines.

Your child might enjoy reading the following books:

Because of Winn-Dixie
by Kate Dicamillo

Call It Courage
by Armstrong Sperry

Mummies, Tombs, and Treasure: Secrets of Ancient Egypt
by Lila Perl

COOK BOOK
by
Denise Salt

_____ **'s Incentive Chart: Week 7**

Name Here

This week, I plan to read_____ minutes each day.

CHART YOUR PROGRESS HERE.

Week 1	Day 1	Day 2	Day 3	Day 4	Day 5
I read for...	minutes	minutes	minutes	minutes	minutes
Put a sticker to show you completed each day's work.					

Congratulations!

Wow! You did a great job this week!

#1

Place sticker here.

Parent or Caregiver's Signature_____

All in a Day's Work

Think about how the first pair of words is related. Then write the word that completes the second part of the analogy. Use the words in the box or another word you know that fits.

conductor	cashier	custodian
astronaut	professor	paratrooper
geologist	architect	archaeologist
hairdresser	physician	astronomer

1. **Spade is to gardener as baton is to** _____.

2. **Athlete is to team as** _____ **is to faculty.**

3. **Lawyer is to courtroom as** _____ **is to salon.**

4. **Pattern is to seamstress as blueprint is to** _____.

5. **Cook is to chef as clean is to** _____.

6. **Scuba is to diver as parachute is to** _____.

7. **Mechanic is to garage as** _____ **is to space station.**

8. **Screwdriver is to carpenter as stethoscope is to** _____.

9. **Books are to librarian as rocks are to** _____.

10. **Flight attendant is to airplane as** _____ **is to supermarket .**

11. **Collector is to taxes as** _____ **is to artifacts.**

12. **Lasso is to cowhand as telescope is to** _____.

Notice the suffixes that end many of the words for people. Knowing that the suffix -er means "one who" can help you figure out the meaning of a word. List the suffixes on this page. Find out what they mean.

Sassy Sentences

A **sentence** is a group of words that expresses a complete thought. When you write a sentence, you put your thoughts into words. If the sentence is complete, the meaning is clear. It contains a subject (the naming part) and a predicate (an action or state of being part).

These are sentences.
Sally sells seashells at the seashore.
Betty Botter bought a bit of better butter.

These are not sentences.
Peck of pickled peppers.
Flying up a flue.

Make complete sentences by adding words to each group of words. Try to create tongue twisters like the sentences above.

1. _____ flips fine flapjacks.

2. **Sixty slippery seals** _____ .

3. _____ fed Ted _____ .

4. **Ruby Rugby's baby brother** _____ .

5. _____ managing an imaginary magazine.

6. **Sam's sandwich shop**_____ .

7. _____ back blue balloons.

8. _____ pink peacock pompously _____ .

9. **Pete's pop Pete** _____ .

10. _____ sawed Mr. Saw's _____ .

11. **A flea and a fly**_____ .

12. _____ black-backed bumblebee.

Create your own tongue twisters to share with friends. Make sure each one expresses a complete thought.

Scholastic Inc. Summer Express: Between Grades 4 & 5

Drizzle with Details

A good paragraph needs supporting sentences that tell more about the main idea of the topic sentence. Supporting sentences are sometimes called detail sentences. Every detail sentence in a paragraph must relate to the main idea. In the following paragraph, the one supporting sentence that does not relate to the main idea has been underlined.

My first day of softball practice was a total disaster! Not only was I ten minutes late, but I also forgot my glove. Then during batting practice, I missed the ball every time I took a swing. <u>I definitely have improved on my catching skills.</u> To make matters even worse, I tripped in the outfield and twisted my ankle. I was definitely not off to a very good start.

Read the following paragraph. Underline the topic sentence. Then cross out any supporting sentences that do not relate to the main idea.

Yesterday our science class went on a field trip to a pond. Next month we're going to the ocean. That will be fun. We've been studying the pond as an ecosystem in class. Our teacher wanted us to observe firsthand all the different habitats in and around the pond. She had us keep a checklist of the different kinds of plants and animals in each pond habitat. One of the boys accidentally fell in. He was really embarrassed. Along the water's edge I saw several kinds of plants partly underwater, two salamanders, snails, and water bugs. I observed many different habitats.

Measure by Measure

Josie is surrounded by all kinds of measuring tools. But she's not sure which tool does what! Sure, she knows that a ruler measures the length of something. But she doesn't realize that all the other tools around her are used for measuring things too. Try giving Josie a hand.

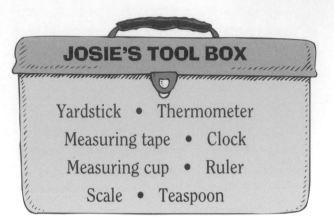

JOSIE'S TOOL BOX

Yardstick • Thermometer

Measuring tape • Clock

Measuring cup • Ruler

Scale • Teaspoon

Directions:

Take a look at the list of measuring tools in Josie's Tool Box. Use the list to answer the questions below.

1. What tool could Josie use to measure the weight of a pumpkin? _____

2. What tool could Josie use to measure the width of her math book?

   _____

3. Josie plans to watch one of her favorite television shows. What tool could help her measure the length of each commercial that appears during that show?

   _____

4. Josie has an awful cough. What tool could she use to measure the amount of cough syrup she should take? _____

5. If Josie's mom wants to find out Josie's temperature, which tool could she use?

   _____

6. Say Josie wanted to make a cake. What tool could she use to measure the milk she needs to put in the cake mix? _____

7. What tool could Josie use to measure the height of her brother's tree house?

   _____

8. What tool could Josie give her dad to measure the length of their living room?

   _____

Choose four of the measuring tools in Josie's Tool Box. Make a list of things you could measure with each of those tools.

Scholastic Inc. Summer Express: Between Grades 4 & 5

Honoring Heroes

Details *in a story provide the reader with information about the main idea and help the reader better understand the story.*

Washington, D.C., is the capital of the United States. It is located between Virginia and Maryland on the Potomac River. Washington, D.C., is also the headquarters of the federal government. This incredible city is a symbol of our country's history and the home of many important historical landmarks.

Many of Washington, D.C.'s famous landmarks are located in the National Mall. The Mall is a long, narrow, parklike area that provides large open spaces in the middle of the city's many huge buildings. In addition to being home to the U.S. Capitol, where Congress meets, and the White House, the Mall is also dedicated to honoring the history of our nation. Memorials for presidents George Washington, Abraham Lincoln, Thomas Jefferson, and Franklin D. Roosevelt can all be found in the Mall. There are also memorials honoring Americans who fought in the Korean and Vietnam Wars.

Near the Lincoln Memorial another memorial was built. It is the National World War II Memorial. This memorial honors Americans who fought and supported the United States during World War II. The U.S. fought in this war from 1941 to 1945.

The memorial's design includes a Rainbow Pool, two giant arches, a ring of stone columns, and a wall covered with gold stars. Each star represents 100 Americans who died while fighting in World War II.

Bob Dole, a former senator and World War II veteran, worked tirelessly to get this memorial built. He believes that the memorial will remind Americans of the value of freedom. "Freedom is not free," says Dole. "It must be earned . . . ."

More than $197 million was raised to build the memorial that means so much to Dole and to many other Americans. Many businesses, private groups, and schools donated money to this cause. The memorial was completed in 2004.

1. Where is Washington, D.C., located? _____

_____

2. Write three facts about Washington, D.C. _____

_____

_____

3. Which four presidents are memorialized in the National Mall? _____

_____

4. Besides the four presidents, who else is honored in the Mall?_____

_____

5. What is the name of the memorial? _____

_____

6. Why was it built? _____

_____

7. How long did the United States fight in World War II? _____

8. What are some features of the new memorial?_____

_____

9. Write what the stars represent. _____

_____

10. What World War II veteran has worked hard trying to get the memorial built? ____

_____

11. What remembrance does Dole think the memorial will bring to the minds

of people? _____

_____

12. What are the sources of the money that was raised to build the memorial? _____

_____

Read about another memorial in Washington, D.C. On another sheet of paper, write five details about the memorial.

Scholastic Inc. *Summer Express: Between Grades 4 & 5*

The Corner Candy Store

 Word problems that suggest equal groups often require multiplication.

Write a number sentence for each problem. Solve.

A. Sam bought 4 candy bars at $1.23 each. How much did Sam spend altogether?	B. Mr. Johnson, the store owner, ordered 48 boxes of jawbreakers. Each box contained 392 pieces of candy. How many jawbreakers did Mr. Johnson order?
C. Carly's mom sent her to the candy store with 29 party bags. She asked Carly to fill each bag with 45 pieces of candy. How many pieces of candy will Carly buy?	D. Thirty-five children visited the candy store after school. Each child spent 57¢. How much money was spent in all?
E. Mr. Johnson keeps 37 jars behind the candy counter. Each jar contains 286 pieces of candy. How many pieces of candy are behind the counter altogether?	F. Nick bought each of his 6 friends a milk shake. Each milk shake cost $2.98. How much did Nick spend in all?

Poems Take Shape

A concrete poem is one that's shaped like its subject matter. Here's an example.

Pizza Pizzaz

Have you even seen a more delicious sight,
Than a pizza dressed up to go out at night?
Thick tomato sauce and mozzarella cheese,
Mushrooms, sausage, more peppers, please!
Onions, olives,   choice pepperoni!
Anything goes, just   hold the anchovies!
Top it all off with   a sprinkle of spice—
It's looking   so good . . .
Hey, who   took a slice?

Now it's your turn. In BOX 1, create a short concrete poem about an umbrella. To get inspired, shut your eyes and imagine that you are an umbrella. How does the rain sound? Are you soaked? Are you lonely? When you're finished, use BOX 2 to design a concrete poem in a shape you choose.

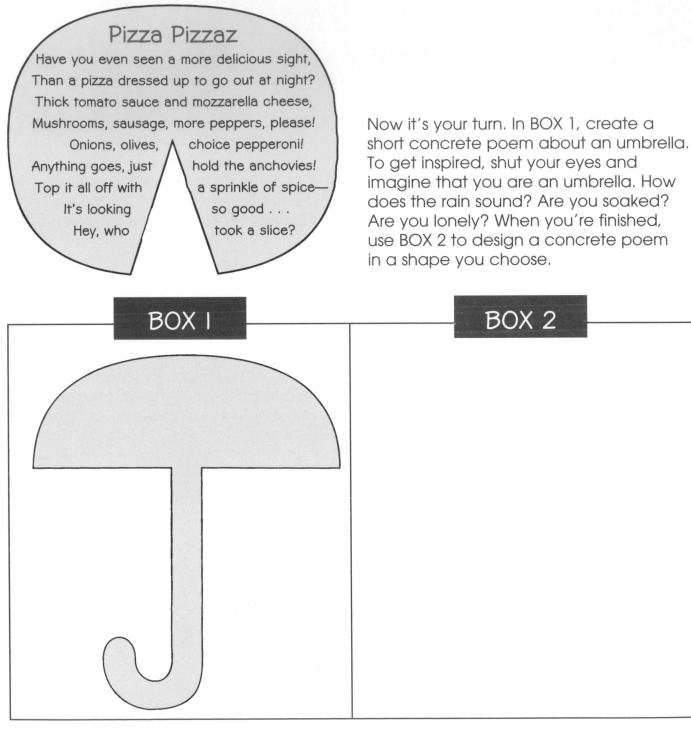

BOX 1

BOX 2

Look for other examples of concrete poems in books of poetry.

Horseplay

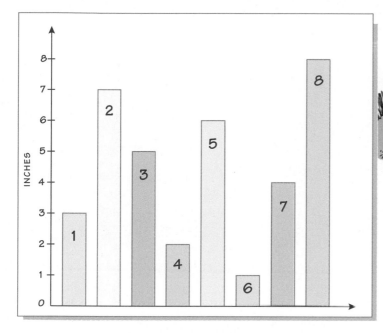

Why did the horse sneeze?

KACHOO!

Decoder

4 bars	T
6 inches	K
bar 5	L
bar 2	A
bar 6	L
2 inches	U
2 bars	P
5 inches	L
bar 8	T
7 inches	W
bar 3	O
bar 1	S
3 inches	E
8 inches	C
8 bars	M
4 inches	T
3 bars	H
bar 4	N
bar 7	I

Answer each question about the graph. Then use the Decoder to solve the riddle by filling in the blanks at the bottom of the page.

1. Which is the tallest bar on the graph? _____

2. Which is the shortest bar on the graph? _____

3. How tall is bar 1? _____

4. How much taller is bar 5 than bar 4? _____

5. How much shorter is bar 4 than bar 2? _____

6. How tall is bar 8? _____

7. Which bar is taller: bar 1 or bar 7? _____

8. Which bar is shorter: bar 2 or bar 3? _____

9. Which bar is twice the size of bar 1? _____

10. How many of bar 4 would equal bar 8? _____

IT HAD A ___ ___ ___ ___ ___ ___ " ___ ___ ___ ___."
2   7   10   4   9   3   6   8   5   1

91

A Musical Lesson

*There are many kinds of paragraphs. When you write a **comparison paragraph**, you compare by telling how things are similar and contrast by telling how things are different. You can use a Venn diagram to help organize your ideas. Here is an example.*

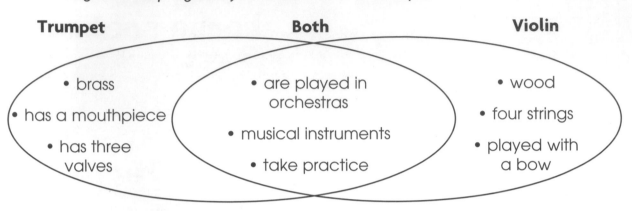

Trumpet
- brass
- has a mouthpiece
- has three valves

Both
- are played in orchestras
- musical instruments
- take practice

Violin
- wood
- four strings
- played with a bow

Complete the paragraph using details to compare and contrast the trumpet and violin. Remember to capitalize and punctuate correctly.

Trumpet Versus Violin

The trumpet and violin are both musical instruments that are _____

_____. However, there are some

important differences. The trumpet _____

_____

_____

_____

On the other hand, the violin _____

_____

_____

Both instruments _____

_____

Make a list on a sheet of paper of things to compare and contrast such as a house and an apartment building, ice skating and skateboarding, or spinach and broccoli. Choose one pair. Make and complete a Venn diagram like the one above. Then write a paragraph to tell how they are similar and different.

Scholastic Inc.   Summer Express: Between Grades 4 & 5

Helping Your Child Get Ready: Week 8

These are the skills your child will be working on this week.

Math
- multiplying decimals and whole numbers
- division facts

Reading
- drawing conclusions

Writing
- distinguishing facts and opinions
- writing a persuasive paragraph

Vocabulary
- synonyms, antonyms, and homophones
- organizing words by their meanings

Grammar
- parts of speech
- commas and colons
- verb tenses

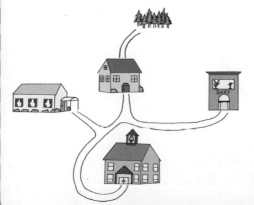

Here are some activities you and your child might enjoy.

Super Summaries Writing a summary is often hard for children. To help your child practice this skill, have him or her practice creating one-sentence summaries of favorite books, movies, or television shows. To do this, have him or her answer this question in just one sentence: Who did what, when, and why? This may take a bit of practice!

Neat Mnemonics Mnemonics are a great way to help kids memorize important information. Share the following spelling mnemonics with your child.

There is **a rat** in sep**arat**e.
and
A princi**pal** can be your **pal**.

Encourage your child to make up other mnemonics to help remember tricky spellings.

Name Acrostic Invite your child to use his or her name to write a descriptive acrostic poem. For example,

> *Awesome*
> *Neat*
> *Near-sighted*
> *Apples*

Cartography 101 Have your child create a map of your neighborhood. Take a walk around the area first, and then have him or her decide what symbols and colors to use to represent various buildings and places.

Your child might enjoy reading the following books:

Titantic
by Victoria Sherrow

Pure Dead Magic
by Deb Gliori

Bridge to Terabithia
by Katherine Paterson

_____'s Incentive Chart: Week 8

Name Here

This week, I plan to read _____ minutes each day.

CHART YOUR PROGRESS HERE.

Week 1	Day 1	Day 2	Day 3	Day 4	Day 5
I read for...	minutes	minutes	minutes	minutes	minutes
Put a sticker to show you completed each day's work.					

Congratulations!

Wow! You did a great job this week!

#1

Place sticker here.

Parent or Caregiver's Signature _____

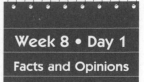
Is That a Fact?

 *What is the difference between a fact and an opinion? A **fact** can be checked or proven. An opinion is what someone believes or feels about something. An **opinion** cannot be proven.*

Fact → **Cocoa beans are used to make chocolate.**
Opinion → **Chocolate pudding is better than chocolate ice cream.**

Read each sentence. Write *F* next to each fact. Write *O* next to each opinion.

_____ 1. **Everyone in the world thinks chocolate makes the best candy.**

_____ 2. **In Switzerland, the average person eats about 22 pounds of chocolate in a year.**

_____ 3. **That means the Swiss eat about 160 million pounds of chocolate annually.**

_____ 4. **I think Americans eat more chocolate than that.**

_____ 5. **People also use chocolate to make drinks and to flavor recipes.**

_____ 6. **There's nothing better than a chocolate donut with chocolate glaze.**

Look at the pictures. Then write two facts and two opinions about each snack food. Use clue words such as *think, best, believe, like,* and *dislike* to signal an opinion.

1. **Fact:** _____

_____

_____

Opinion: _____

_____

_____

2. **Fact:** _____

_____

_____

Opinion: _____

_____

_____

3. **Fact:** _____

_____

_____

Opinion: _____

_____

_____

As you listen to a conversation among your friends about an issue that is important to them, try to identify the facts and opinions you hear and write them down on a sheet of paper. Then ask, "Can this statement be proven?" If the answer is yes, then it is a fact. If not, then it is an opinion. Circle any clue words or phrases that signal opinions.

Oh, My Aching Heart!

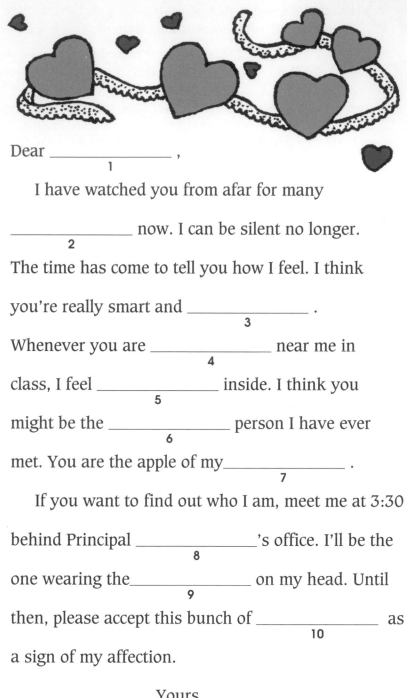

Don't read this story yet! Give it to a partner and ask him or her to tell you the parts of speech under the blanks below. You give a word for each part of speech, and your partner writes it in the blank. Then he or she writes the words in the story and reads the story aloud.

1. _____
   FRIEND'S NAME

2. _____
   PLURAL UNIT OF TIME

3. _____
   ADJECTIVE

4. _____
   VERB ENDING IN *ING*

5. _____
   ADJECTIVE

6. _____
   ADJECTIVE ENDING IN *EST*

7. _____
   BODY PART

8. _____
   CELEBRITY'S LAST NAME

9. _____
   NOUN

10. _____
    PLURAL NOUN

11. _____
    ADVERB

12. _____
    ADJECTIVE

13. _____
    ADJECTIVE ENDING IN *ER*

14. _____
    VERB

Dear _____ ,
                1

I have watched you from afar for many

_____ now. I can be silent no longer.
        2

The time has come to tell you how I feel. I think

you're really smart and _____ .
                              3

Whenever you are _____ near me in
                        4

class, I feel _____ inside. I think you
                  5

might be the _____ person I have ever
                    6

met. You are the apple of my_____ .
                                    7

   If you want to find out who I am, meet me at 3:30

behind Principal _____'s office. I'll be the
                        8

one wearing the_____ on my head. Until
                      9

then, please accept this bunch of _____ as
                                        10

a sign of my affection.

                    Yours _____ ,
                                11

                    Your _____ admirer
                              12

P.S. It is _____ to _____ and
              13   14

lose than never to love at all.

Scholastic Inc.   *Summer Express: Between Grades 4 & 5*

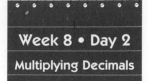

A Smart Butterfly

When multiplying with decimals, place the decimal point in the product, counting from right to left, the same number of places as the sum of the decimal places in the factors.

$6.95
x   3
The decimal point is 2 places, counting from right to left, in the top factor. There is no decimal point in the bottom factor. 2 + 0 = 2

$6.95
x   3
$20.85
Place the decimal point 2 places, counting from right to left, in the product.

Multiply. Then use the code to answer the riddle below.

I.	**E.**	**A.**	**T.**	**W.**	**O.**
2.8	26.5	32.8	20.41	0.24	0.04
x 3	x 4	x 7	x 5	x 9	x 8

H.	**S.**	**I.**	**T.**	**I.**	**M.**
3.06	300.1	24.81	24.6	41.5	0.416
x 6	x 8	x 6	x 5	x 3	x 5

T.	**M.**	**C.**	**N.**	**A.**	**A.**
45.6	48.5	4.53	3.08	3.49	6.94
x 8	x 3	x 3	x 4	x 7	x 9

Why did the butterfly learn decimals?

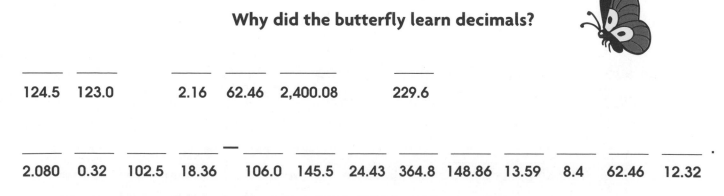

___	___		___	___	___		___	
124.5	123.0		2.16	62.46	2,400.08		229.6	

___	___	___	___	—	___	___	___	___	___	___	___	___	___	.
2.080	0.32	102.5	18.36		106.0	145.5	24.43	364.8	148.86	13.59	8.4	62.46	12.32	

Word Wise

Each word below has a synonym, an antonym, and a homophone. See how many you know and can list without referring to the word box at the bottom of the page.

	Synonym	Antonym	Homophone
1. stationary			
2. taut			
3. current			
4. alter			
5. banned			
6. bolder			
7. coarse			
8. cruel			
9. sum			
10. sheer			
11. birth			
12. attendance			

Word box:

loose	some	still	rough	origin	thin	total	prohibited
presence	taught	altar	maintain	outdated	absence	up-to-date	
death	meeker	thick	boulder	band	tight	attendants	
berth	smooth	change	braver	permitted	course	difference	
moving	shear	currant	kind	hurtful	crewel	stationery	

Make a chart like the one above for new words. Here are some to get you started.

cheap   build   brake   compliment   die   hire   tow   foul   sweet

Scholastic Inc.   Summer Express: Between Grades 4 & 5

On the Move

Sam and Danny cannot believe that they have to move away from Florida. Florida is so awesome! They can play outside all day long—every day. It is almost always warm and sunny, and all of their friends live there. What will they do without Brendan, Bailey, John, Alexis, and Brian? They will never have such great friends again. Never!

However, Sam and Danny are very excited for their dad. He has a great new job. The only problem is that the job is in New Hampshire. Danny was not even sure where this state was located. After learning that it is way up north near Canada, both boys did get a little excited about playing in the snow. Danny has always wanted to learn to ski, and Sam thinks playing ice hockey sounds like fun.

Sam and Danny also like the location of New Hampshire. It is between Maine and Vermont and not far from Boston, Massachusetts. Quebec, Canada, borders this state on the north. Neither of the boys has ever visited this part of the country, so they are now looking forward to exploring a new area. If only their friends could come with them! Their parents have promised that they can visit their old friends over spring break and even go to Disney World. The boys think that moving to New Hampshire will not be so bad after all.

1. **How do Sam and Danny feel about Florida?** _____

   _____

2. **Circle how Sam and Danny feel about leaving their friends.**
   They are sad.
   They do not know what they will do without their good friends.
   They know they will make a lot of new friends.

3. **Circle how the boys feel about moving to New Hampshire.**
   They think it sounds like a fun, interesting part of the country.
   They are excited about visiting their old friends on spring break.
   They are disappointed that it is next to Vermont.

4. **On the map above, label New Hampshire and the country and states that border it.**

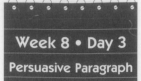

I'm Convinced!

In a **persuasive paragraph,** *you give an opinion about something and try to convince readers to think or feel the way you do. A convincing persuasive paragraph includes*

— **a topic sentence that clearly states your opinion.**
— **reasons that support your opinion.**
— **facts to back up your opinion.**
— **a strong closing sentence that summarizes your opinion.**

Pretend you are a world famous chef who prepares dishes that include edible insects—insects that you can eat. You want to persuade people to include insects in their diet. Here is a topic sentence for a persuasive paragraph.

Everyone should try cooking with insects.

Here are some reasons and facts.
• Many insects like mealworms, crickets, and weevils are edible.
• People in many cultures around the world eat insects.
• Many insects are low in fat and rich in vitamins.
• Lots of tasty recipes include insects.
• Insects are really quite delicious.

Now put it all together. Write a persuasive paragraph that includes a title and a strong closing sentence. Remember the rules for writing a paragraph.

Paragraph Title: _____

Topic Sentence: _____

_____

_____

Reasons/Facts: _____

_____

_____

_____

_____

_____

_____

Closing Sentence: _____

_____

Scholastic Inc.   Summer Express: Between Grades 4 & 5

Television Division

Each part of a division problem has a name.

$$5 \leftarrow \text{quotient}$$

$$\text{divisor} \rightarrow 9\,\overline{)\,45} \leftarrow \text{dividend}$$

Divide.

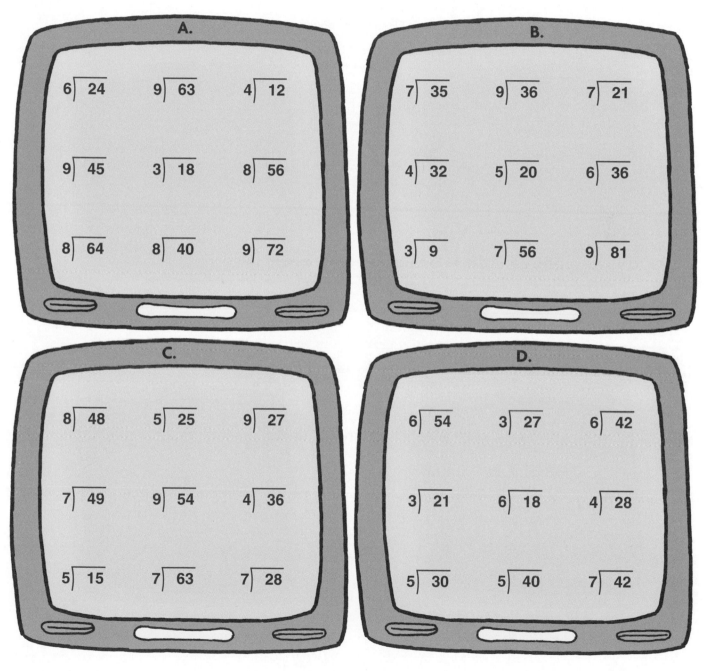

A.

$6\,\overline{)\,24}$	$9\,\overline{)\,63}$	$4\,\overline{)\,12}$
$9\,\overline{)\,45}$	$3\,\overline{)\,18}$	$8\,\overline{)\,56}$
$8\,\overline{)\,64}$	$8\,\overline{)\,40}$	$9\,\overline{)\,72}$

B.

$7\,\overline{)\,35}$	$9\,\overline{)\,36}$	$7\,\overline{)\,21}$
$4\,\overline{)\,32}$	$5\,\overline{)\,20}$	$6\,\overline{)\,36}$
$3\,\overline{)\,9}$	$7\,\overline{)\,56}$	$9\,\overline{)\,81}$

C.

$8\,\overline{)\,48}$	$5\,\overline{)\,25}$	$9\,\overline{)\,27}$
$7\,\overline{)\,49}$	$9\,\overline{)\,54}$	$4\,\overline{)\,36}$
$5\,\overline{)\,15}$	$7\,\overline{)\,63}$	$7\,\overline{)\,28}$

D.

$6\,\overline{)\,54}$	$3\,\overline{)\,27}$	$6\,\overline{)\,42}$
$3\,\overline{)\,21}$	$6\,\overline{)\,18}$	$4\,\overline{)\,28}$
$5\,\overline{)\,30}$	$5\,\overline{)\,40}$	$7\,\overline{)\,42}$

On another sheet of paper, write nine division facts with a quotient of 8.

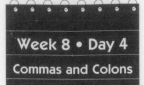

Commas and Colons

Commas are used to separate items in a series, to separate parts of dates, to separate parts of names when the last name is written first, and to follow the greeting and closing of letters. **Colons** are used to separate hours and minutes in expressions of time, to introduce a list, and to follow the greeting of a business letter.

A. **Answer the questions, paying careful attention to your use of commas and colons.**

1. Write your name and the names of two classmates as they would appear on an official document.

   _____

   _____

   _____

2. What is your date of birth? _____

3. What time does your school begin? _____ end? _____

B. **Read each sentence. Add a comma or colon where needed. Write *correct* if the sentence is correct.**

1. Luke Sam and Nick are putting on a play.

2. The play will begin at 800 PM.

3. Yalixa his sister wrote the play.

4. They will perform the play Wednesday and Thursday.

5. Amy can you make the costumes?

6. Like her mom Luisa is a good singer.

7. Our flag is red white and blue.

8. Michael plays baseball and soccer.

9. Nathan will visit on March 28 2004.

10. We are always happy when he comes but sad when he leaves.

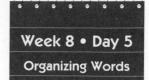

Inside Information

Look at the items in column A of the chart below. Every one of them is commonly found *inside* one item in column B. Match the appropriate pairs and write your answers on the blanks below. There is only one correct letter match for each numbered item. We've done the first one for you.

COLUMN A	COLUMN B	CORRECT MATCH
1. butter	a. balloon	__1. e__
2. coin	b. pantry	_____
3. pupil	c. vault	_____
4. pig	d. shed	_____
5. helium	e. refrigerator	_____
6. cereal	f. sty	_____
7. assets	g. fountain	_____
8. rake	h. eye	_____
9. license	i. bottle	_____
10. arrow	j. mirror	_____
11. battery	k. flashlight	_____
12. mercury	l. quiver	_____
13. reflection	m. thermometer	_____
14. lint	n. wallet	_____
15. message	o. dryer	_____

YOUR TURN

Think of five more items commonly found inside another item, as in the chart above. Mix them up and see if someone in your family can pair them together correctly.

Scholastic Inc.   Summer Express: Between Grades 4 & 5

Grammar Cop
and the Case of the Emperor's New Clothes

The emperor doesn't know if he's coming or going! He doesn't know what he has done, what he is doing now, and what he will do later. Can you help Grammar Cop choose the right tense?

Decide whether each underlined verb is in the past, present, or future tense. Write it in the blank.

_____ 1. There <u>will be</u> a big parade next week.

_____ 2. I <u>have</u> nothing to wear.

_____ 3. I <u>asked</u> the tailors to make me a new cloak.

_____ 4. They <u>promised</u> to make the best cloak the villagers had ever seen.

_____ 5. The tailors <u>are working</u> day and night cutting and sewing.

_____ 6. The cloak <u>is finished</u>!

_____ 7. I <u>tried</u> it on, and something was very strange . . . .

_____ 8. But the tailors assured me that the townspeople <u>will be amazed</u>.

_____ 9. After the parade, all the people <u>said</u> they had never seen anything like my new cloak.

_____ 10. I <u>tried</u> to find the tailors to thank them, but they had left town.

Remember these basic laws of tenses:

• Past
The past tense of a verb tells that something already happened. (Example: I **walked** to school this morning.)

• Present
The present tense of a verb tells that something is happening now. (Example: It **is raining** today.)

• Future
The future tense of a verb tells that something will happen in the future. (Example: Tomorrow I **will play** soccer.)

Scholastic Inc. Summer Express: Between Grades 4 & 5

These are the skills your child will be working on this week.

Math
- division with remainders
- division with decimals
- changing decimals to fractions

Reading
- main ideas and supporting details

Writing
- writing an expository paragraph
- using exact verbs

Vocabulary
- syllabication

Grammar
- proofreading
- dialogue and quotation marks

Here are some activities you and your child might enjoy.

20 Questions The game of 20 Questions is a great way to build thinking skills. Choose a category (such as animals). Think of one animal. Tell your child he or she can ask only "yes" or "no" questions to determine what animal you're thinking of. Once he or she gets the hang of it, take turns asking questions.

Local Historians Have your child research the history of your community. Have him or her find out the name of the Indians who lived in the area, the first Europeans to arrive, the oldest house or building, and the origin of your community's name.

Numbers That Name You There are lots of numbers that label, count, measure, or order information about a person. For example, everyone has a birthday and an address. Ask your child to think about all the numbers that relate to him or her and list them on a sheet of paper.

Make a Word Play this simple word game. Have your child see how many words he or she can make from the letters in the word *Washington*.

Your child might enjoy reading the following books:

Rosa Parks: From the Back of the Bus to the Front of a Movement
by Cammie Wilson

Encyclopedia Brown
by Donald J. Sobol

Charlie and the Chocolate Factory
by Roald Dahl

Washington

as
was
in
to
sing

ton
wash
ash
won
saw

_____'s Incentive Chart: Week 9

This week, I plan to read _____ minutes each day.

CHART YOUR PROGRESS HERE.

Week 1	Day 1	Day 2	Day 3	Day 4	Day 5
I read for...	minutes	minutes	minutes	minutes	minutes
Put a sticker to show you completed each day's work.					

Congratulations!

Wow! You did a great job this week!

#1

Place sticker here.

Parent or Caregiver's Signature _____

Honeycomb

Solve the problems. If the answer has a remainder between 1 and 4, color the shape yellow. If the answer has a remainder between 5 and 8, color the shape blue. Finish the design by coloring the other shapes with the colors of your choice.

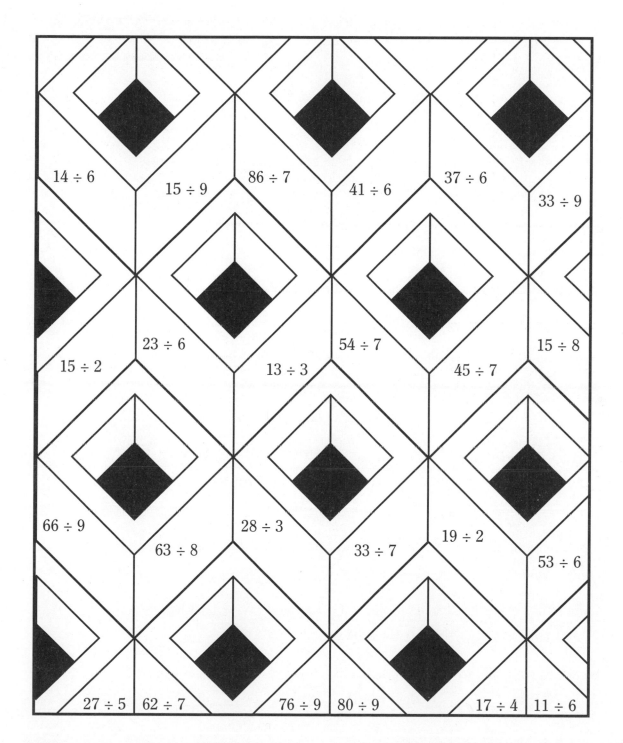

$14 \div 6$ $15 \div 9$ $86 \div 7$ $41 \div 6$ $37 \div 6$ $33 \div 9$

$15 \div 2$ $23 \div 6$ $13 \div 3$ $54 \div 7$ $45 \div 7$ $15 \div 8$

$66 \div 9$ $63 \div 8$ $28 \div 3$ $33 \div 7$ $19 \div 2$ $53 \div 6$

$27 \div 5$ $62 \div 7$ $76 \div 9$ $80 \div 9$ $17 \div 4$ $11 \div 6$

Syllable Wizardry

How good are you at building words and figuring out how many syllables they have? Answer these tricky and fun questions about words to find out. Some questions may have more than one answer. Write your answers in the blanks.

TIPS
- No answers are proper nouns.
- No answers are foreign words.
- Do not rearrange or subtract any letters from the given word to form the new word.

1. What letter can you add to "eve" to make it a common *two*-syllable word?

  Letter _____ New word _____

2. What letter can you add to "sleep" to make it a common *two*-syllable word?

  Letter _____ New word _____

3. What letter can you add to "rise" to make it a common *two*-syllable word?

  Letter _____ New word _____

4. What letter can you add to "rode" to make it a common *two*-syllable word?

  Letter _____ New word _____

5. What letter can you add to "rode" to make it a common *three*-syllable word?

  Letter _____ New word _____

6. What letter can you add to "man" to make it a common *two*-syllable word?

  Letter _____ New word _____

7. What letter can you add to "are" to make it a common *three*-syllable word?

  Letter _____ New word _____

8. What letter can you add to "pen" to make it a common *two*-syllable word?

  Letter _____ New word _____

9. What letter can you add to "came" to make it a common *two*-syllable word?

  Letter _____ New word _____

10. What letter can you add to "came" to make it a common *three*-syllable word?

  Letter _____ New word _____

Scholastic Inc.   Summer Express: Between Grades 4 & 5

Step by Step

When you write an **expository paragraph**, you give facts and information, explain ideas, or give directions. An expository paragraph can also include opinions. Here are some topic ideas for an expository paragraph.

Explain how to play the flute.
Tell why you do not like brussels sprouts.
Give facts about yourself.

Explain how to bathe a dog.
Tell what skills you need to skateboard.
Give the facts about your favorite band.

Here is an example of an expository paragraph. It explains how to fry an egg.

Frying an egg is not all that difficult. After melting a little bit of butter in a frying pan, just crack the eggshell along the rim of the pan and let the egg drop into the pan. Do it gently so the yolk does not break. Let the egg fry over a low heat for about a minute or so. That is all it takes.

Complete the following topics for expository paragraphs with your own ideas.

Explain how to	Give facts about	Tell why
_____	_____	_____
_____	_____	_____
_____	_____	_____

Use the form below to develop one of your ideas for an expository paragraph.

Paragraph Title: _____

Topic Sentence: _____

_____

Details/Facts/Steps: _____

_____

_____

_____

_____

Closing Sentence: _____

Now, use the plan above to write a paragraph on a sheet of paper. If you are giving directions for doing or making something, include words such as *first, next, after that,* and *finally* to make the steps clear for your readers.

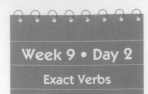

Action Alert

 When you write, think about the verbs that you choose to express action in your sentences. Are they as exact as they can be? Do they tell your readers exactly what you want to say?

*The child **broke** the plastic toy.*
*The child **smashed** the plastic toy.*
*The child **cracked** the plastic toy.*

Each verb creates a different picture of what happened.

Read each sentence. Underline the verb. Then rewrite each sentence using a more exact verb. You may want to use a thesaurus.

1. **Three young hikers went up the steep hill.**

   _____

2. **A lone runner ran around the track.**

   _____

3. **The wind blew through the treetops.**

   _____

4. **The janitor cleaned the scuff marks off the floor.**

   _____

5. **The audience laughed at the hilarious scene.**

   _____

6. **The diners ate the delicious meal.**

   _____

7. **The young tourists liked the castle most of all.**

   _____

8. **The children slept for about an hour.**

   _____

9. **The biologist looked at the unusual specimen.**

   _____

Here are some commonly used verbs: make, tell, say, speak, ride. On a sheet of paper, list as many exact verbs as you can think of for each one. Use a thesaurus for additional words. Then write several sentences using the exact words on your list.

Scholastic Inc.   Summer Express: Between Grades 4 & 5

Dialogue and Quotations

Quotation marks are used to show the beginning and end of someone's exact words. An **indirect quotation** is a summary of what someone has written or said. Quotation marks are not used in indirect quotes.

A. **In each sentence, underline the words that the speaker or speakers actually said. Then add quotation marks where they belong.**

1. Can't we stay up just five more minutes? the children begged.

2. Kate replied, That's another story.

3. What's for lunch? Bob asked.

4. I am so excited! Betsy cried.

B. **The following dialogue is missing commas, question marks, and other necessary punctuation. Write the correct punctuation on each line.**

1. Poissant said__ "I remember once when Duke Ellington stayed at my house__"

2. "Was Duke Ellington famous__" Punkin asked__

3. "He sure was__" Miss Ida exclaimed__

4. "I not only met him__" Poissant explained__ "but I was sitting in the parlor when he sat down at the piano and started to play__"

C. **All the punctuation, including quotation marks, is missing from this dialogue. Write the missing punctuation marks on the lines.**

1. __Duke's playing sure heated up that little room____ exclaimed Poissant__

2. __Did any other famous people stay at your house____ asked Freda__

3. __No____ said Poissant____but Lena Horne once stayed at Miss Jackson's house____

4. Then he added__ __However__ that is a story for another day____

Ride the Wave of Decimal Division

 Sometimes zeros are needed in the quotient. When dividing decimals by a whole number, follow these steps.

$$
\begin{array}{r}
2\\
27\overline{)55.08}\\
-54\\
\hline
1
\end{array}
$$

1. Divide the whole number.

$$
\begin{array}{r}
2.\\
27\overline{)55.08}\\
-54\\
\hline
1
\end{array}
$$

2. Place the decimal point in the quotient.

$$
\begin{array}{r}
2.0\\
27\overline{)55.08}\\
-54\\
\hline
10\ (<27)
\end{array}
$$

3. Bring down the 0. Since it is still < 27, place a zero in the quotient.

$$
\begin{array}{r}
2.04\\
27\overline{)55.08}\\
-54\\
\hline
108\\
-108\\
\hline
0
\end{array}
$$

4. Bring down the 8. Divide into 108.

Divide. Then write the letter for each quotient from least to greatest on the lines below to learn where the 1958 megatsunami occurred.

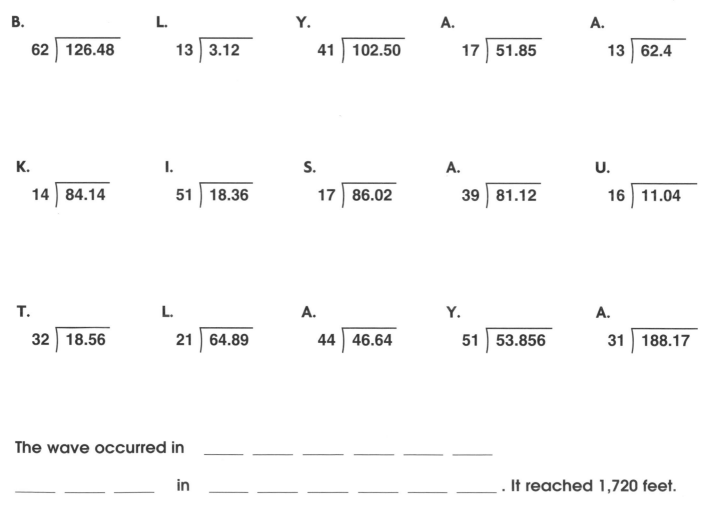

B. $62\overline{)126.48}$

L. $13\overline{)3.12}$

Y. $41\overline{)102.50}$

A. $17\overline{)51.85}$

A. $13\overline{)62.4}$

K. $14\overline{)84.14}$

I. $51\overline{)18.36}$

S. $17\overline{)86.02}$

A. $39\overline{)81.12}$

U. $16\overline{)11.04}$

T. $32\overline{)18.56}$

L. $21\overline{)64.89}$

A. $44\overline{)46.64}$

Y. $51\overline{)53.856}$

A. $31\overline{)188.17}$

The wave occurred in ____ ____ ____ ____ ____

____ ____ ____ **in** ____ ____ ____ ____ ____ ____ . **It reached 1,720 feet.**

Scholastic Inc.   *Summer Express: Between Grades 4 & 5*

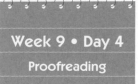

Proofing Pays

Capitalization and end punctuation help show where one sentence ends and the next one begins. Whenever you write, proofread to make sure each sentence begins with a capital letter and ends correctly. Here's an example of how to mark the letters that should be capitalized.

have you ever heard of a Goliath birdeater? it is
the world's largest spider. this giant tarantula can grow
to 11 inches in length and weigh about 6 ounces. now that's
a big spider! although it is called a birdeater, it usually
eats small reptiles and insects. these spiders are
mostly found in rain forests.

Read the passage below. It is about another amazing animal, but it is not so easy to read because the writer forgot to add end punctuation and to use capital letters at the beginning of sentences. Proofread the passage. Mark the letters that should be capitals with the capital letter symbol. Put the correct punctuation marks at the ends of sentences. Then reread the passage.

think about the fastest car you've ever seen in the Indianapolis 500 race

that's about how fast a peregrine falcon dives it actually reaches speeds up

to 175 miles an hour that's incredibly fast peregrine falcons are also very

powerful birds did you know that they can catch and kill their prey in the air

using their sharp claws what's really amazing is that peregrine falcons live in

both the country and in the city keep on the lookout if you're ever in New York

City believe it or not, it is home to a very large population of falcons

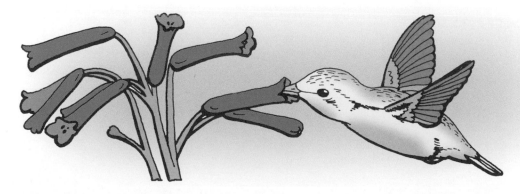

What do you know about the bee hummingbird, atlas moth, or capybara? Choose one, do some research, and write several sentences about it on a sheet of paper. Then proofread your writing. Does every sentence begin and end correctly? Are all the words spelled correctly?

Triangular Patterns

To change a decimal to a fraction, use the greatest common factor to reduce to lowest terms.

$$0.8 = \frac{8 \div 2}{10 \div 2} = \frac{4}{5} \qquad 0.40 = \frac{40 \div 20}{100 \div 20} = \frac{2}{5} \qquad 0.250 = \frac{250 \div 250}{1,000 \div 250} = \frac{1}{4}$$

Using a ruler, draw a line to match each decimal with its fraction.

See how many triangles you can find in the diagram.

Eating in Egypt

Suppose you lived thousands of years ago in Ancient Egypt. What would you have eaten? Like all Ancient Egyptians, you would eat bread with every meal. Garlic bread, raisin bread, and nutbread were three favorites. Egyptians also ate a lot of fruit including figs, dates, and pomegranates. Vegetables were also part of their diet. Lettuce, beans, onions, cucumbers, and leeks were all popular. How do you think you'd like your Egyptian meal?

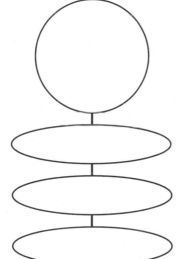

Write the topic and three subtopics on the web. Complete the web by writing details for each subtopic.

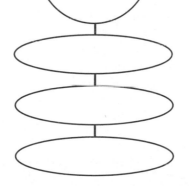

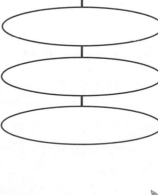

Write down everything you eat in one day.

Testing It Out

Use after completing Eating in Egypt on page 115.

Fill in the circle of the best answer.

1. **One kind of food that Ancient Egyptians ate at every meal was—**
   - Ⓐ lettuce
   - Ⓒ bread
   - Ⓑ figs
   - Ⓓ eggs

2. **Ancient Egyptians often ate fruit called—**
   - Ⓐ leeks
   - Ⓒ apples
   - Ⓑ beans
   - Ⓓ dates

3. **A food group that includes onions is—**
   - Ⓐ grains
   - Ⓒ vegetables
   - Ⓑ meat
   - Ⓓ cheese

4. **Because Ancient Egyptians made raisin bread, you can guess they grew—**
   - Ⓐ grapes
   - Ⓒ pomegranates
   - Ⓑ bread
   - Ⓓ cucumbers

5. **From this passage, you can guess that Ancient Egyptians—**
   - Ⓐ hunted animals
   - Ⓒ raised chickens
   - Ⓑ grew crops
   - Ⓓ fished in the sea

6. **One kind of tree that most likely grew in Egypt was the—**
   - Ⓐ fig tree
   - Ⓒ oak tree
   - Ⓑ bean tree
   - Ⓓ pine tree

7. **Because they had fruit, you can guess that Ancient Egyptians probably—**
   - Ⓐ raised bees
   - Ⓒ drank milk
   - Ⓑ drank juices
   - Ⓓ ate potatoes

8. **A food that the passage does not mention is—**
   - Ⓐ vegetables
   - Ⓒ fruit
   - Ⓑ nuts
   - Ⓓ meat

Scholastic Inc.   Summer Express: Between Grades 4 & 5

Helping Your Child Get Ready: Week 10

These are the skills your child will be working on this week.

Math
- equivalent fractions
- plotting coordinates
- decimals, fractions, and percents

Reading
- determining cause and effect
- standardized reading test practice

Writing
- proofreading

Vocabulary
- analogies

Grammar
- possessives
- commas

Here are some activities you and your child might enjoy.

Create a Moon Calendar Have your child track the moon's changes for a month. Get or make a calendar for the month that has large boxes. Each night, go outside with your child to look at the moon, and then have him or her draw its shape in that day's box.

Listen Up Help your child build listening and memorizing skills with this activity. Have him or her listen carefully as you read and reread the list of Great Lakes below. Then ask your child to repeat it back to you in the same order.

Lake Superior, Lake Huron, Lake Michigan, Lake Erie, and Lake Ontario

Riddle Me This Show your child how to make up number riddles. Read the following riddle to your child as a model:

> I am an even number.
> I am the number of outs made in a full,
> 9-inning baseball game.
> I am the product of 6 times 3 times 3.

Once he or she gets the hang of it, have your child create riddles for you to answer.

Pet Autobiography Suggest that your child write the story of your pet's (or an imaginary pet's) life. The story should be an autobiography—that is, told from the pet's point of view!

Your child might enjoy reading the following books:

Great Whales: The Gentle Giants
by Patricia Lauber

The Color of My Words
by Lynn Joseph

Math Potatoes
by Greg Tang

This week, I plan to read_____minutes each day.

CHART YOUR PROGRESS HERE.

Week 1	Day 1	Day 2	Day 3	Day 4	Day 5
I read for...	minutes	minutes	minutes	minutes	minutes
Put a sticker to show you completed each day's work.					

Congratulations!

Wow! You did a great job this week!

#1

Place sticker here.

Parent or Caregiver's Signature_____

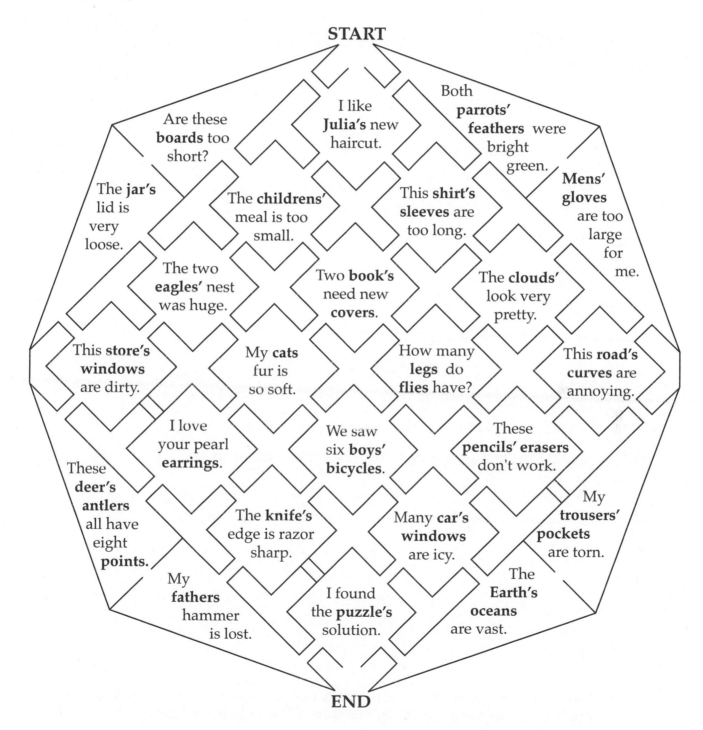

Maze

Find the path to the end by passing only through spaces containing words in **bold** that are correctly spelled. The shortest path will take you through 15 spaces with correct spellings.

START

Are these **boards** too short?

I like **Julia's** new haircut.

Both **parrots' feathers** were bright green.

The **jar's** lid is very loose.

The **childrens'** meal is too small.

This **shirt's** sleeves are too long.

Mens' gloves are too large for me.

The two **eagles'** nest was huge.

Two **book's** need new **covers**.

The **clouds'** look very pretty.

This **store's windows** are dirty.

My **cats** fur is so soft.

How many **legs** do **flies** have?

This **road's curves** are annoying.

I love your pearl **earrings**.

We saw six **boys' bicycles**.

These **pencils' erasers** don't work.

These **deer's antlers** all have eight **points**.

The **knife's** edge is razor sharp.

Many **car's windows** are icy.

My **trousers' pockets** are torn.

My **fathers** hammer is lost.

I found the **puzzle's** solution.

The **Earth's oceans** are vast.

END

Scholastic Inc. Summer Express: Between Grades 4 & 5

Comma Capers

You know that you must use commas in a series of three or more items.
Max, Sam, and Alex ordered burgers, fries, and milkshakes for lunch.

Here are some additional rules you need to know about commas.
Use commas

— *to set off the name of the person or group you are addressing.*
Here's your order, boys.

— *after words like* yes, no, *and* well.
Well, what do you want to do now?

— *before a conjunction that joins two sentences.*
The boys finished lunch, and then they went to a movie.

Read the sentences below. Decide which ones need commas and which ones do not.
Use this symbol ⋏ to show where commas belong.

1. **I'd like a bike a pair of in-line skates and a snowboard for my birthday.**

2. **Well my friend you can't always have what you want when you want it.**

3. **No but I can always hope!**

4. **My friends and I skate all year long and snowboard during the winter.**

5. **I used to like skateboarding but now I prefer snowboarding and in-line skating.**

6. **What sports games or hobbies do you enjoy most Jody?**

7. **I learned to ski last year and now I'm taking ice-skating lessons.**

8. **Skiing ice skating and skateboarding are all fun things to do.**

Review the four rules above for using commas. Then write an original sentence for
each rule. Begin and end each sentence correctly. Remember to check your spelling.

9. _____

10. _____

11. _____

12. _____

Writers use commas for other reasons. As you read a newspaper, an article in your favorite magazine, a letter, or a book, look for examples of commas in sentences and jot them down on a sheet of paper. Then see if you can figure out the rules.

Scholastic Inc.   Summer Express: Between Grades 4 & 5

Fractions Are a Breeze

Sail into fractions by renaming each fraction below in lowest terms.

If the fraction is equal to 1/2 or 3/4, shade the box blue.

If the fraction is equal to 1/4, shade the box yellow.

If the fraction is equal to 1/3, shade the box green.

If the boxes are colored correctly, a picture will appear.

$\frac{3}{6}$	$\frac{2}{8}$	$\frac{21}{42}$	$\frac{75}{150}$	$\frac{31}{62}$	$\frac{11}{22}$	$\frac{7}{14}$
$\frac{50}{100}$	$\frac{9}{36}$	$\frac{11}{44}$	$\frac{32}{64}$	$\frac{30}{60}$	$\frac{6}{12}$	$\frac{60}{120}$
$\frac{4}{8}$	$\frac{7}{28}$	$\frac{16}{64}$	$\frac{3}{12}$	$\frac{8}{16}$	$\frac{40}{80}$	$\frac{12}{16}$
$\frac{9}{18}$	$\frac{25}{100}$	$\frac{6}{24}$	$\frac{8}{32}$	$\frac{19}{76}$	$\frac{48}{64}$	$\frac{5}{10}$
$\frac{10}{20}$	$\frac{17}{68}$	$\frac{12}{48}$	$\frac{13}{52}$	$\frac{20}{80}$	$\frac{25}{100}$	$\frac{14}{28}$
$\frac{35}{70}$	$\frac{8}{32}$	$\frac{10}{40}$	$\frac{15}{60}$	$\frac{40}{160}$	$\frac{14}{56}$	$\frac{5}{20}$
$\frac{21}{28}$	$\frac{12}{24}$	$\frac{40}{80}$	$\frac{15}{30}$	$\frac{33}{66}$	$\frac{15}{20}$	$\frac{75}{100}$
$\frac{5}{10}$ $\frac{2}{6}$	$\frac{12}{36}$	$\frac{9}{27}$	$\frac{30}{90}$	$\frac{20}{60}$	$\frac{11}{33}$	$\frac{6}{18}$ $\frac{2}{4}$
$\frac{18}{24}$ $\frac{9}{12}$	$\frac{5}{15}$	$\frac{15}{45}$	$\frac{8}{24}$	$\frac{10}{30}$	$\frac{3}{9}$ $\frac{6}{8}$	$\frac{30}{40}$

Bon Voyage!

Moonwalkers on City Streets

Do you need some exercise? Do you want to see some city sights? Perhaps you want to assert your rights as a pedestrian in a city designed for cars. Then you might want to join a group called Moonwalkers in Bethlehem, Pennsylvania. The Moonwalkers meet once a week at night. Then they stride through their city, up hills, down streets, over bridges, and along canals. What are some other reasons that people enjoy moonwalking? They get to meet other members of their community, and they enjoy being out at night.

Find five causes and one effect in the passage.
Write them on the map.

Causes   **Effect**

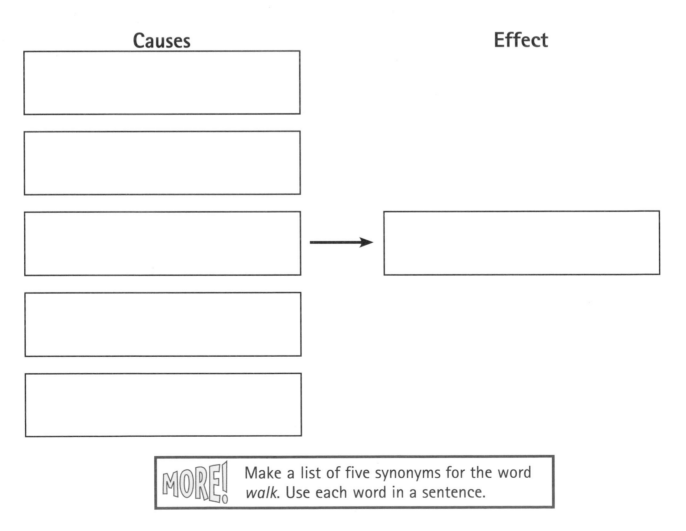

MORE! Make a list of five synonyms for the word *walk*. Use each word in a sentence.

What's Hoppin'?

You Answer It!

1. Look at the graph below. Starting at square X, Judy hopped 4 squares up and 3 squares to the right. In which square did she land?

_____

NOTE: Judy and Rudy can hop in vertical and horizontal directions only.

4. Find the 2 shortest paths to get from square X to square D.

_____

_____

5. Find 3 paths to get from square D to square E. Does each path contain the same total number of squares?

_____

_____

2. Rudy is in square X. Which are the 2 shortest paths he can take to get to square E?

_____

_____

3. Judy is in square A. Which are the 2 shortest paths she can take to get to square E?

_____

_____

6. Starting at square X, Rudy hopped 6 squares up and 5 squares to the left. How many squares is he from square D?

_____

_____

Stories Behind Inventions That Changed the World
(That May or May Not Be True)

Find and mark the eleven spelling errors.

The Jacket Zipper

The first zipper, the Model 100-A, was made of solid wood and weyed over 17 ponds. Over time, the size decreased. Metal replased wood. A solid gold zipper weighed in at only 4.1 ownces. Unfortunatelly, it cost over $1,500. Finally, the Model 100-Z came out. It was a lot like the zipper of today—except two people were required to zip it up.

The Bookmark

Ted E. Bear, in a 1997 interview, discloseed, "I kept loosing my place in the book I was reading. I tried putting a peece of cheese in there, but it was greasy. I tried a giant rock. It was too heavy and awkward. I tried a $100 bill. It worked well, but that was all the money I had! Finally, I tried a small slip of paper. At last, the bookmark was born!

The Cereal Spoon

First, people tried to eat cereal with their hands. What a mess! There was milk driping from everyone's elbows. Next, a garden shovel was tried. Too big! It was replaced with a fork. The size was good, but it leaked. Finally, someone pulled out a spoon. There was little chance after so many faillurs that it would work. But it was perfect!

Beekeeping Basics

Open a jar of golden honey. Spread some on a slice of toast. Take a bite and enjoy its special sweetness. There's nothing else quite like it!

Where does honey come from? Bees make it, right? But wait! Bees are insects. They don't set up little factories for making honey and putting it in jars, do they? What's the real story behind the honey we eat?

Since ancient times, people have known that bees make a delicious, sweet food. To get it, people would search for a hive of wild bees and steal the honey. Then some people figured out that they could get honey more easily if they made hives for bees to live in. They became beekeepers.

The first hives were probably hollow logs or clay pots turned on their sides. Later, in about 1500, farmers in Europe began building straw beehives that looked like baskets turned upside down. Farmers from Europe brought honeybees with them to America in the 1600s.

Around 1850, an American beekeeper invented a better kind of hive called the *hanging movable-frame beehive*. It looks like a stack of boxes. Inside are wooden frames where bees build wax honeycombs for storing their honey. This is the kind of hive that most beekeepers use today.

The amazing thing about a beehive is how much it actually *is* like a little factory for making honey. Each hive is home to a colony of as many as 60,000 bees. A colony has one queen that lays eggs. Other bees have different jobs, such as building the honeycomb, keeping it clean, feeding the young, or making honey. Some bees are guards that protect the hive. If a guard thinks you are a danger to the colony, it will sting you.

Honey is made from *nectar*, a sweet liquid inside flowers. A bee sucks nectar from a flower and then brings it back to the hive. A wax-making bee places the nectar in a honey cell. Other bees add more and more nectar to the honey cell. The nectar is mostly water when it is first brought to the hive. "House bees" fan their wings over the cell to remove the water. As the water evaporates, the nectar changes into honey. When the honey in a cell is ready, the bees cover it with a wax cap.

Beekeepers give the bees several months to fill the honeycombs in a hive. Bees must gather nectar from more than a million flowers to make just one pound of honey! When the honey is ready to harvest, beekeepers wear special clothes that cover their bodies completely. Otherwise, they would surely be stung many times as they pull frames filled with honey from the hive.

Using special tools, beekeepers can extract the honey without breaking the honeycomb. They do this so that the bees will not need to rebuild the honeycomb. When the beekeeper puts the frames back into the hive, the bees will start filling them with honey again.

No bee can make honey alone. It takes a large team of very hard workers to get the job done. We could learn a lot from these little creatures about working together and getting things done.

1. **Beekeepers extract honey without breaking the honeycomb. What does extract mean?**
   Ⓐ take out   Ⓒ make
   Ⓑ fill up   Ⓓ eat

2. **How is a beehive like a factory?**

   _____

   _____

   _____

3. **List four steps in the making of honey.**

   _____

   _____

   _____

   _____

4. **Which sentence best states the main idea of this article?**
   Ⓕ Be careful around honeybees—they sting!
   Ⓖ An American invented the best kind of beehive.
   Ⓗ Honeybees are useful and interesting creatures.
   Ⓙ Beekeepers have been around for a long time.

Scholastic Inc.   Summer Express: Between Grades 4 & 5

Identifying Relationships

Write the phrase from the box that tells how the first two words are related.
Then write the correct word to complete the analogy.

Relationship:	Same Class	Part/Whole	Synonyms
	Antonyms	Homophones	

1. weight : wait :: gilt : _____   Relationship _____
   (A) wave   (B) guilt   (C) gill

2. work : play :: deep : _____   Relationship _____
   (A) shallow   (B) dive   (C) job

3. elm : pine :: bee : _____   Relationship _____
   (A) birch   (B) honey   (C) beetle

4. seam : seem :: I : _____   Relationship _____
   (A) me   (B) eye   (C) you

5. kernel : corn :: seed : _____   Relationship _____
   (A) soil   (B) water   (C) watermelon

6. forest : woods :: field : _____   Relationship _____
   (A) meadow   (B) flower   (C) farmer

7. leave : arrive :: asked : _____   Relationship _____
   (A) go   (B) told   (C) inquired

8. wheel : we'll :: hall : _____   Relationship _____
   (A) help   (B) hill   (C) haul

Explain to someone in your family how you chose each answer.

Free-Throw Percents

Hoops, Dunk'n, and Shooter are on the court again! How do their numbers add up? Follow the steps below to make sense of their percents.

1. Hoops took 10 free throws and made 4. What percent did he make?

    4/10 = _____/100 = _____%

2. Dunk'n took 4 free throws and made 3.

    a. What fraction did he make? _____ = _____/100

    b. What fractions did he miss? _____ = _____/100

    c. What percent did he make? _____%

    d. What percent did he miss? _____%

3. Shooter took 20 free throws and made 13.

    a. What fraction did he make? _____

    b. What fraction did he miss? _____

    c. What percent did he make? _____

    d. What percent did he miss? _____

All-Star Math!

4. Hoops makes 60 percent of the free throws he takes.

    a. In lowest terms, what fraction of free throws did he make? _____

    b. If he took 10 free throws, how many should he make? _____

    c. If he took 15 free throws, how many should he make? _____

    d. If he took 200 free throws, how many should he make? _____

Remember!

Percents are fractions of 100.
For example: 25/100 = 25%
Or 3/25 = 12/100 = 12%

Scholastic Inc. Summer Express: Between Grades 4 & 5

Answer Key

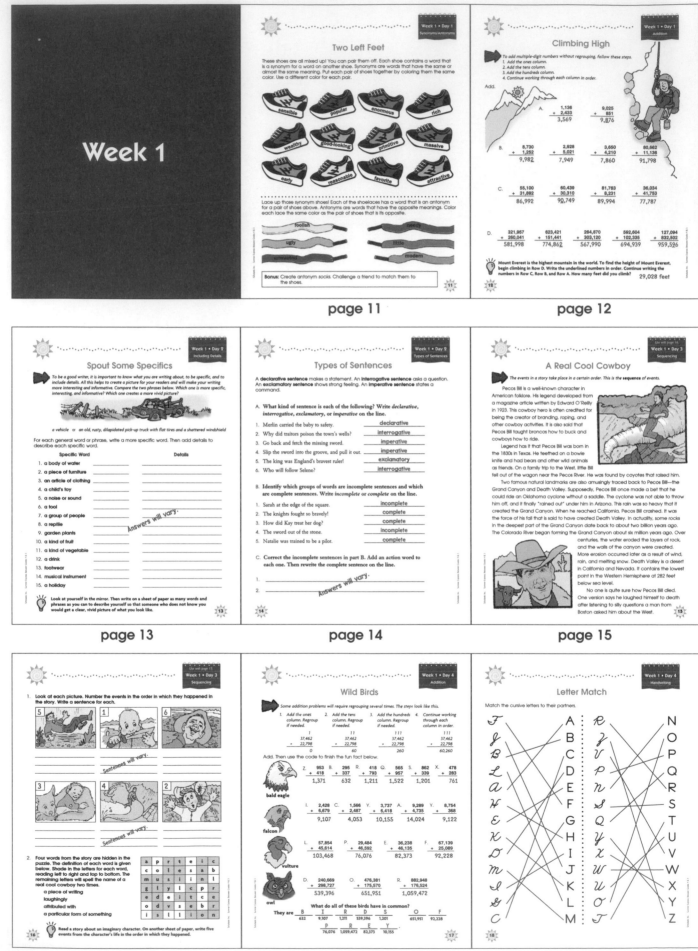

Week 1

---

page 11

Two Left Feet

These shoes are all mixed up! You can pair them off. Each shoe contains a word that is a synonym for a word on another shoe. Synonyms are words that have the same or almost the same meaning. Put each pair of shoes together by coloring them the same color. Use a different color for each pair.

sensible   popular   enormous   rich
wealthy   good-looking   primitive   massive
early   reasonable   favorite   attractive

Lace up those synonym shoes! Each of the shoelaces has a word that is an antonym for a pair of shoes above. Antonyms are words that have the opposite meanings. Color each lace the same color as the pair of shoes that is its opposite.

foolish   needy
ugly   little
unwanted   modern

Bonus: Create antonym socks. Challenge a friend to match them to the shoes.

---

page 12

Climbing High

To add multiple-digit numbers without regrouping, follow these steps.
1. Add the ones column.
2. Add the tens column.
3. Add the hundreds column.
4. Continue working through each column in order.

Add.

A.
$1,136 + 2,433 = 3,569$
$9,025 + 851 = 9,876$

B.
$8,730 + 1,252 = 9,982$
$2,928 + 5,021 = 7,949$
$3,650 + 4,210 = 7,860$
$80,662 + 11,136 = 91,798$

C.
$55,100 + 31,892 = 86,992$
$60,439 + 30,310 = 90,749$
$81,763 + 8,231 = 89,994$
$36,034 + 41,753 = 77,787$

D.
$321,957 + 260,041 = 581,998$
$623,421 + 151,441 = 774,862$
$264,870 + 303,120 = 567,990$
$592,604 + 102,335 = 694,939$
$127,094 + 832,502 = 959,596$

Mount Everest is the highest mountain in the world. To find the height of Mount Everest, begin climbing in Row D. Write the underlined numbers in order. Continue writing the numbers in Row C, Row B, and Row A. How many feet did you climb?   **29,028 feet**

---

page 13

Spout Some Specifics

To be a good writer, it is important to know what you are writing about, to be specific, and to include details. All this helps to create a picture for your readers and will make your writing more interesting and informative. Compare the two phrases below. Which one is more specific, interesting, and informative? Which one creates a more vivid picture?

a vehicle or *an old, rusty, dilapidated pick-up truck with flat tires and a shattered windshield*

For each general word or phrase, write a more specific word. Then add details to describe each specific word.

Specific Word	Details
1. a body of water	
2. a piece of furniture	
3. an article of clothing	
4. a child's toy	
5. a noise or sound	
6. a tool	
7. a group of people	
8. a reptile	
9. garden plants	
10. a kind of fruit	
11. a kind of vegetable	
12. a drink	
13. footwear	
14. musical instrument	
15. a holiday	

Answers will vary.

Look at yourself in the mirror. Then write on a sheet of paper as many words and phrases as you can to describe yourself so that someone who does not know you would get a clear, vivid picture of what you look like.

---

page 14

Types of Sentences

A **declarative sentence** makes a statement. An **interrogative sentence** asks a question. An **exclamatory sentence** shows strong feeling. An **imperative sentence** states a command.

A. What kind of sentence is each of the following? Write *declarative, interrogative, exclamatory,* or *imperative* on the line.

1. Merlin carried the baby to safety.   declarative
2. Why did traitors poison the town's wells?   interrogative
3. Go back and fetch the missing sword.   imperative
4. Slip the sword into the groove, and pull it out.   imperative
5. The king is England's bravest ruler!   exclamatory
6. Who will follow Selene?   interrogative

B. Identify which groups of words are incomplete sentences and which are complete sentences. Write *incomplete* or *complete* on the line.

1. Sarah at the edge of the square.   incomplete
2. The knights fought so bravely!   complete
3. How did Kay treat her dog?   complete
4. The sword out of the stone.   incomplete
5. Natalie was trained to be a pilot.   complete

C. Correct the incomplete sentences in part B. Add an action word to each one. Then rewrite the complete sentence on the line.

1. _____
2. _____
Answers will vary.

---

page 15

A Real Cool Cowboy

The events in a story take place in a certain order. This is the **sequence of events.**

Pecos Bill is a well-known character in American folklore. His legend developed from a magazine article written by Edward O'Reilly in 1923. This cowboy hero is often credited for being the creator of branding, roping, and other cowboy activities. It is also said that Pecos Bill taught broncos how to buck and cowboys how to ride.

Legend has it that Pecos Bill was born in the 1830s in Texas. He teethed on a bowie knife and had bears and other wild animals as friends. On a family trip to the West, little Bill fell out of the wagon near the Pecos River. He was found by coyotes that raised him.

Two famous natural landmarks are also amusingly traced back to Pecos Bill—the Grand Canyon and Death Valley. Supposedly, Pecos Bill once made a bet that he could ride an Oklahoma cyclone without a saddle. The cyclone was not able to throw him off, and it finally "rained out" under him in Arizona. This rain was so heavy that it created the Grand Canyon. When he reached California, Pecos Bill crashed. It was the force of his fall that is said to have created Death Valley. In actuality, some rocks in the deepest part of the Grand Canyon date back to about two billion years ago. The Colorado River began forming the Grand Canyon about six million years ago. Over centuries, the water eroded the layers of rock, and the walls of the canyon were created. More erosion occurred later as a result of wind, rain, and melting snow. Death Valley is a desert in California and Nevada. It contains the lowest point in the Western Hemisphere at 282 feet below sea level.

No one is quite sure how Pecos Bill died. One version says he laughed himself to death after listening to silly questions a man from Boston asked him about the West.

---

page 16

1. Look at each picture. Number the events in the order in which they happened in the story. Write a sentence for each.

5   1   6
3   4   2

Sentences will vary.

2. Four words from the story are hidden in the puzzle. The definition of each word is given below. Shade in the letters for each word, reading left to right and top to bottom. The remaining letters will spell the name of a real cool cowboy two times.

a	p	r	t	e	i	c
c	o	l	e	s	a	b
m	u	s	i	i	n	l
g	l	y	l	c	p	r
e	d	e	i	t	c	e
o	d	v	s	e	b	r
i	s	t	l	l	i	o	n

a piece of writing
laughingly
attributed with
a particular form of something

Read a story about an imaginary character. On another sheet of paper, write five events from the character's life in the order in which they happened.

---

page 17

Wild Birds

Some addition problems will require regrouping several times. The steps look like this.

1. Add the ones column. Regroup if needed.
2. Add the tens column. Regroup if needed.
3. Add the hundreds column. Regroup if needed.
4. Continue working through each column in order.

$37,462 + 22,798$ → $60,260$

Add. Then use the code to finish the fun fact below.

Z. $953 + 418 = 1,371$ B. $295 + 337 = 632$ R. $418 + 793 = 1,211$ Q. $565 + 957 = 1,522$ S. $862 + 339 = 1,201$ X. $478 + 283 = 761$
bald eagle

I. $2,428 + 6,679 = 9,107$ C. $1,566 + 2,487 = 4,053$ Y. $3,737 + 6,418 = 10,155$ A. $9,289 + 4,735 = 14,024$ Y. $8,754 + 368 = 9,122$
falcon

L. $57,854 + 45,614 = 103,468$ P. $29,484 + 46,592 = 76,076$ E. $36,238 + 46,135 = 82,373$ F. $67,139 + 25,089 = 92,228$
vulture

D. $240,669 + 298,727 = 539,396$ O. $476,381 + 175,570 = 651,951$ R. $882,948 + 176,524 = 1,059,472$
owl

What do all of these birds have in common?

They are
B I R D S   O F
632 9,107 1,371 539,396 1,201   651,951 92,228

P R E Y .
76,076 1,059,472 82,373   10,155

---

page 18

Letter Match

Match the cursive letters to their partners.

F B L A H E K O M I G C | A B C D E F G H I J K L M
R U V P n S Q Y X W T | N O P Q R S T U V W X Y Z

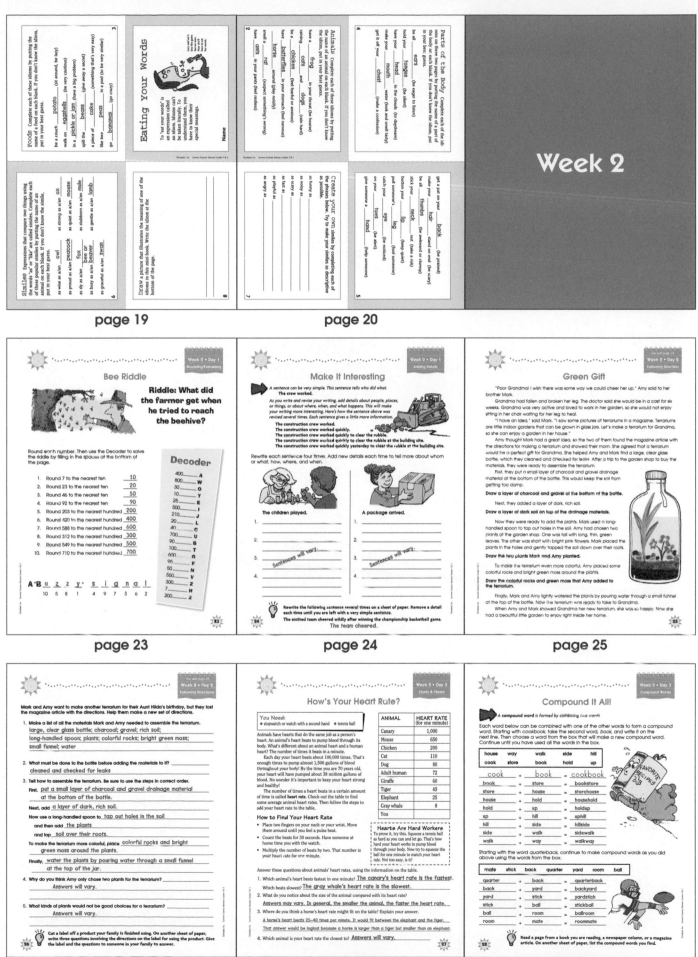

Week 2

page 19

page 20

page 23

page 24

page 25

page 26

page 27

page 28

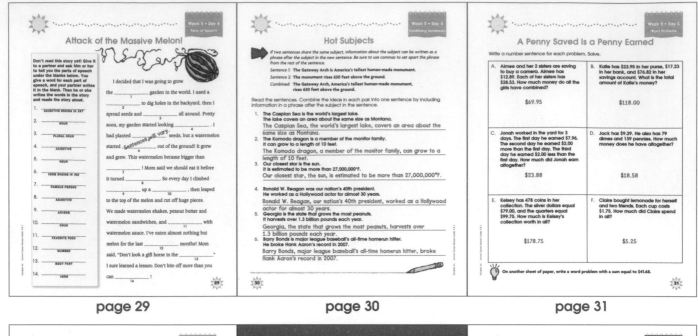

page 29   page 30   page 31

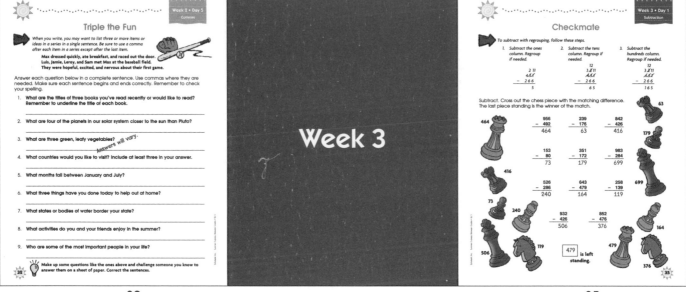

page 32   page 35

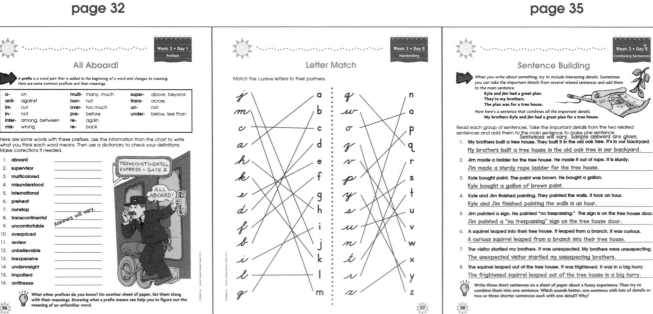

page 36   page 37   page 38

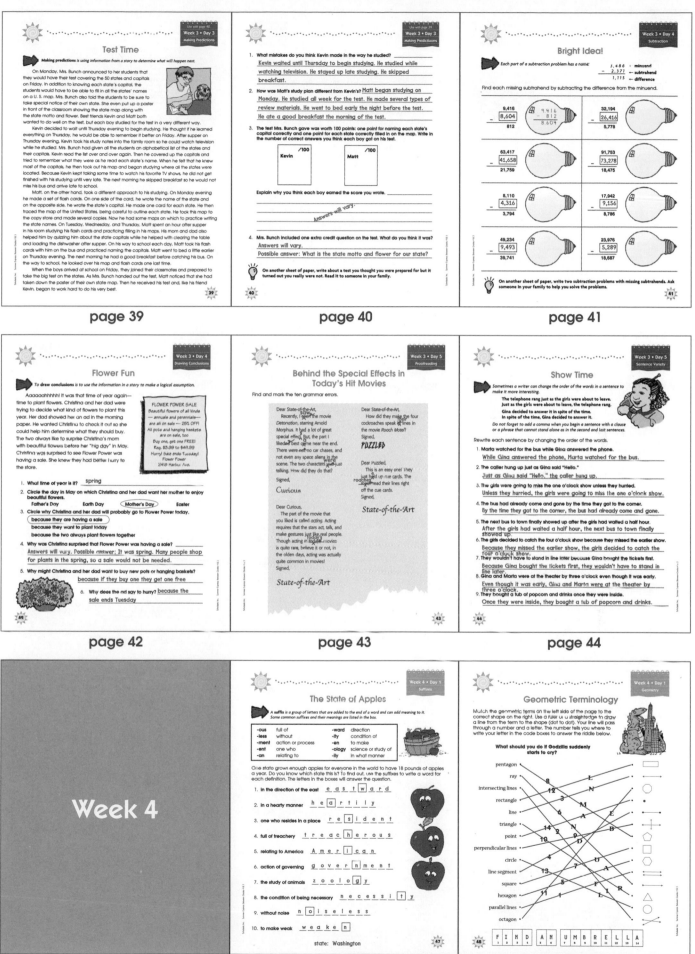

page 39

Test Time

Making predictions is using information from a story to determine what will happen next.

On Monday, Mrs. Bunch announced to her students that they would have their test covering the 50 states and capitals on Friday. In addition to knowing each state's capital, the students would have to be able to fill in all the states' names on a U.S. map. Mrs. Bunch also told the students to be sure to take special notice of their own state. She even put up a poster in front of the classroom showing the state map along with the state motto and flower. Best friends Kevin and Matt both wanted to do well on the test, but each boy studied for the test in a very different way.

Kevin decided to wait until Thursday evening to begin studying. He thought if he learned everything on Thursday, he would be able to remember it better on Friday. After supper on Thursday evening, Kevin took his study notes into the family room so he could watch television while he studied. Mrs. Bunch had given all the students an alphabetical list of the states and their capitals. Kevin read the list over and over again. Then he covered up the capitals and tried to remember what they were as he read each state's name. When he felt that he knew most of the capitals, he then took out his map and began studying where all the states were located. Because Kevin kept taking some time to watch his favorite TV shows, he did not get finished with his studying until very late. The next morning he skipped breakfast so he would not miss his bus and arrive late to school.

Matt, on the other hand, took a different approach to his studying. On Monday evening he made a set of flash cards. On one side of the card, he wrote the name of the state and on the opposite side, he wrote the state's capital. He made one card for each state. He then traced the map of the United States, being careful to outline each state. He took the map to the copy store and made several copies. Now he had some maps on which to practice writing the state names. On Tuesday, Wednesday, and Thursday, Matt spent an hour after supper in his room studying his flash cards and practicing filling in his maps. His mom and dad also helped him by quizzing him about the state capitals while he helped with clearing the table and loading the dishwasher after supper. On his way to school each day, Matt took his flash cards with him on the bus and practiced naming the capitals. Matt went to bed a little earlier on Thursday evening. The next morning he had a good breakfast before catching his bus. On the way to school, he looked over his map and flash cards one last time.

When the boys arrived at school on Friday, they joined their classmates and prepared to take the big test on the states. As Mrs. Bunch handed out the test, Matt noticed that she had taken down the poster of their own state map. Then he received his test and, like his friend Kevin, began to work hard to do his very best.

page 40

1. What mistakes do you think Kevin made in the way he studied?
   Kevin waited until Thursday to begin studying. He studied while watching television. He stayed up late studying. He skipped breakfast.

2. How was Matt's study plan different from Kevin's? Matt began studying on Monday. He studied all week for the test. He made several types of review materials. He went to bed early the night before the test. He ate a good breakfast the morning of the test.

3. The test Mrs. Bunch gave was worth 100 points: one point for naming each state's capital correctly and one point for each state correctly filled in on the map. Write in the number of correct answers you think each boy got on his test.

   Kevin _____ /100   Matt _____ /100

   Explain why you think each boy earned the score you wrote.
   Answers will vary.

4. Mrs. Bunch included one extra credit question on the test. What do you think it was?
   Answers will vary.
   Possible answer: What is the state motto and flower for our state?

On another sheet of paper, write about a test you thought you were prepared for but it turned out you really were not. Read it to someone in your family.

page 41

Bright Idea!

Each part of a subtraction problem has a name:

$$\begin{array}{r} 3,486 \\ -\ 2,371 \\ \hline 1,115 \end{array}$$ ← minuend
← subtrahend
← difference

Find each missing subtrahend by subtracting the difference from the minuend.

9,416 − 8,604 = 812	9,416 − 812 = 8,604	32,194 − 26,416 = 5,778
63,417 − 41,658 = 21,759		91,753 − 73,278 = 18,475
8,110 − 4,316 = 3,794		17,942 − 9,156 = 8,786
49,234 − 9,493 = 39,741		23,976 − 5,289 = 18,687

On another sheet of paper, write two subtraction problems with missing subtrahends. Ask someone in your family to help you solve the problems.

page 42

Flower Fun

To draw conclusions is to use the information in a story to make a logical assumption.

Aaaaaahhhhh! It was that time of year again— time to plant flowers. Christina and her dad were trying to decide what kind of flowers to plant this year. Her dad showed her an ad in the morning paper. He wanted Christina to check it out so she could help him determine what they should buy. The two always like to surprise Christina's mom with beautiful flowers before her "big day" in May. Christina was surprised to see Flower Power was having a sale. She knew they had better hurry to the store.

FLOWER POWER SALE
Beautiful flowers of all kinds
— annuals and perennials —
are all on sale — 25% OFF!
All pots and hanging baskets
are on sale, too.
Buy one, get one FREE!
Reg. $3.99 to $49.99
Hurry! Sale ends Tuesday!
Flower Power
2410 Harbor Ave.

1. What time of year is it?   spring

2. Circle the day in May on which Christina and her dad want their mother to enjoy beautiful flowers.
   Father's Day   Earth Day   (Mother's Day)   Easter

3. Circle why Christina and her dad will probably go to Flower Power today.
   (because they are having a sale)
   because they want to plant today
   because the two always plant flowers together

4. Why was Christina surprised that Flower Power was having a sale?
   Answers will vary. Possible answer: It was spring. Many people shop for plants in the spring, so a sale would not be needed.

5. Why might Christina and her dad want to buy new pots or hanging baskets?
   because if they buy one they get one free

6. Why does the ad say to hurry? because the sale ends Tuesday

page 43

Behind the Special Effects in Today's Hit Movies

Find and mark the ten grammar errors.

Dear State-of-the-Art,
   Recently, I saw the movie Detonation, starring Arnold Morphus. It had a lot of great special effect. But, the part I liked best came near the end. There were no car chases, and not even any space aliens in the scene. The two characters were just talking. How did they do that?
Signed,
Curious

Dear Curious,
   The part of the movie that you liked is called acting. Acting requires that the stars act, talk, and make gestures just like real people. Though acting in today's movies is quite rare, believe it or not, in the olden days, acting was actually quite common in movies!
Signed,
State-of-the-Art

Dear State-of-the-Art,
   How did they make the four cockroaches speak their lines in the movie Roach Motel?
Signed,
PUZZLED

Dear Puzzled,
   This is an easy one! They just held up cue cards. The roaches read their lines right off the cue cards.
Signed,
State-of-the-Art

page 44

Show Time

Sometimes a writer can change the order of the words in a sentence to make it more interesting.

The telephone rang just as the girls were about to leave.
Just as the girls were about to leave, the telephone rang.
Gina decided to answer it in spite of the time.
In spite of the time, Gina decided to answer it.

Do not forget to add a comma when you begin a sentence with a clause or a phrase that cannot stand alone as in the second and last sentences.

Rewrite each sentence by changing the order of the words.

1. Marta watched for the bus while Gina answered the phone.
   While Gina answered the phone, Marta watched for the bus.

2. The caller hung up just as Gina said "Hello."
   Just as Gina said "Hello," the caller hung up.

3. The girls were going to miss the one o'clock show unless they hurried.
   Unless they hurried, the girls were going to miss the one o'clock show.

4. The bus had already come and gone by the time they got to the corner.
   By the time they got to the corner, the bus had already come and gone.

5. The next bus to town finally showed up after the girls had waited a half hour.
   After the girls had waited a half hour, the next bus to town finally showed up.

6. The girls decided to catch the four o'clock show because they missed the earlier show.
   Because they missed the earlier show, the girls decided to catch the four o'clock show.

7. They wouldn't have to stand in line later because Gina bought the tickets first.
   Because Gina bought the tickets first, they wouldn't have to stand in line later.

8. Gina and Marta were at the theater by three o'clock even though it was early.
   Even though it was early, Gina and Marta were at the theater by three o'clock.

9. They bought a tub of popcorn and drinks once they were inside.
   Once they were inside, they bought a tub of popcorn and drinks.

Week 4

page 47

The State of Apples

A suffix is a group of letters that are added to the end of a word and can add meaning to it. Some common suffixes and their meanings are listed in the box.

-ous	full of	-ward	direction
-less	without	-ity	condition of
-ment	action or process	-en	to make
-ent	one who	-ology	science or study of
-an	relating to	-ly	in what manner

One state grows enough apples for everyone in the world to have 18 pounds of apples a year. Do you know which state this is? To find out, use the suffixes to write a word for each definition. The letters in the boxes will answer the question.

1. in the direction of the east   e a s t w a r d
2. in a hearty manner   h e a r t i l y
3. one who resides in a place   r e s i d e n t
4. full of treachery   t r e a c h e r o u s
5. relating to America   A m e r i c a n
6. action of governing   g o v e r n m e n t
7. the study of animals   z o o l o g y
8. the condition of being necessary   n e c e s s i t y
9. without noise   n o i s e l e s s
10. to make weak   w e a k e n

state: Washington

page 48

Geometric Terminology

Match the geometric terms on the left side of the page to the correct shape on the right. Use a ruler or a straightedge to draw a line from the term to the shape (dot to dot). Your line will pass through a number and a letter. The number tells you where to write your letter in the code boxes to answer the riddle below.

What should you do if Godzilla suddenly starts to cry?

pentagon
ray
intersecting lines
rectangle
line
triangle
point
perpendicular lines
circle
line segment
square
hexagon
parallel lines
octagon

F I N D   A N   U M B R E L L A

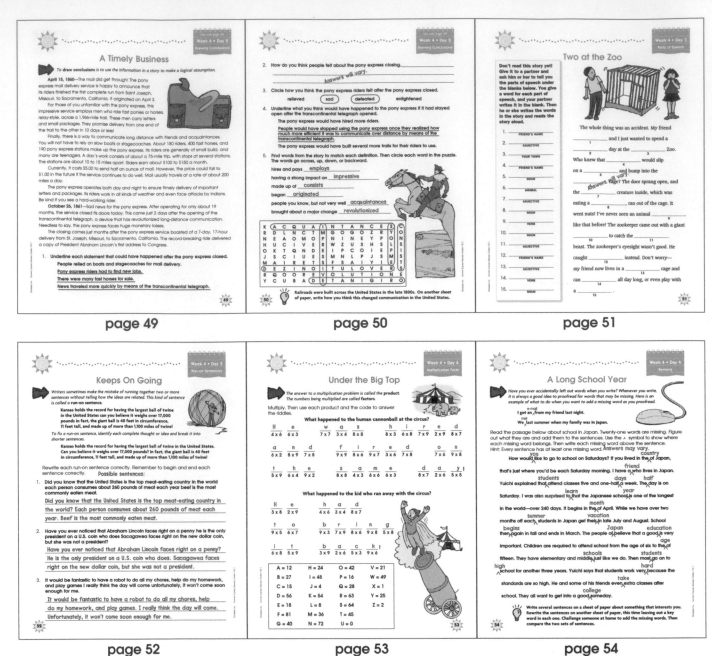

page 49

A Timely Business

To draw conclusions is to use the information in a story to make a logical assumption.

April 15, 1860—The mail did get through! The pony express mail delivery service is happy to announce that its riders finished the first complete run from Saint Joseph, Missouri, to Sacramento, California. It originated on April 3.

For those of you unfamiliar with the pony express, this impressive service employs men who ride fast ponies or horses, relay-style, across a 1,966-mile trail. These men carry letters and small packages. They promise delivery from one end of the trail to the other in 10 days or less!

Finally, there is a way to communicate long distance with friends and acquaintances. You will not have to rely on slow boats or stagecoaches. About 180 riders, 400 fast horses, and 190 pony express stations make up the pony express. Its riders are generally of small build, and many are teenagers. A day's work consists of about a 75-mile trip, with stops at several stations. The stations are about 10 to 15 miles apart. Riders earn about $100 to $150 a month.

Currently, it costs $5.00 to send half an ounce of mail. However, the price could fall to $1.00 in the future if the service continues to do well. Mail usually travels at a rate of about 200 miles a day.

The pony express operates both day and night to ensure timely delivery of important letters and packages. Its riders work in all kinds of weather and even face attacks by Indians. Be kind if you see a hard-working rider.

October 26, 1861—Sad news for the pony express. After operating for only about 19 months, the service closed its doors today. This came just 2 days after the opening of the transcontinental telegraph, a device that has revolutionized long-distance communication. Needless to say, the pony express faces huge monetary losses.

The closing comes just months after the pony express service boasted of a 7-day, 17-hour delivery from St. Joseph, Missouri, to Sacramento, California. The record-breaking ride delivered a copy of President Abraham Lincoln's first address to Congress.

1. Underline each statement that could have happened after the pony express closed.
People relied on boats and stagecoaches for mail delivery.
Pony express riders had to find new jobs.
There were many fast horses for sale.
News traveled more quickly by means of the transcontinental telegraph.

page 50

2. How do you think people felt about the pony express closing. _Answers will vary._

3. Circle how you think the pony express riders felt after the pony express closed.
relieved   sad   defeated   enlightened

4. Underline what you think would have happened to the pony express if it had stayed open after the transcontinental telegraph opened.
The pony express would have hired more riders.
People would have stopped using the pony express once they realized how much more efficient it was to communicate over distance by means of the transcontinental telegraph.
The pony express would have built several more trails for their riders to use.

5. Find words from the story to match each definition. Then circle each word in the puzzle. The words go across, up, down, or backward.
hires and pays   _employs_
having a strong impact on   _impressive_
made up of   _consists_
began   _originated_
people you know, but not very well   _acquaintances_
brought about a major change   _revolutionized_

Railroads were built across the United States in the late 1800s. On another sheet of paper, write how you think this changed communication in the United States.

page 51

Two at the Zoo

Don't read this story yet! Give it to a partner and ask him or her to tell you the parts of speech under the blanks below. You give a word for each part of speech. Your partner writes it in the blank. Then he or she writes the words in the story and reads the story aloud.

1. FRIEND'S NAME
2. ADJECTIVE
3. YOUR TOWN
4. FRIEND'S NAME
5. NOUN
6. ANIMAL
7. ADJECTIVE
8. NOUN
9. VERB
10. NOUN
11. ADJECTIVE
12. FRIEND'S NAME
13. ADJECTIVE
14. VERB
15. NOUN

The whole thing was an accident. My friend ___1___ and I just wanted to spend a ___2___ day at the ___3___ Zoo. Who knew that ___4___ would slip on a ___5___ and bump into the ___6___ cage? The door sprang open, and the ___7___ creature inside, which was eating a ___8___, ran out of the cage. It went nuts! I've never seen an animal ___9___ like that before! The zookeeper came out with a giant ___10___ to catch the ___11___ beast. The zookeeper's eyesight wasn't good. He caught ___12___ instead. Don't worry—my friend now lives in a ___13___ cage and can ___14___ all day long, or even play with ___15___.

page 52

Keeps On Going

Writers sometimes make the mistake of running together two or more sentences without telling how the ideas are related. This kind of sentence is called a run-on sentence.

Kansas holds the record for having the largest ball of twine in the United States can you believe it weighs over 17,000 pounds it is 40 feet in circumference, 11 feet tall, and made up of more than 1,100 miles of twine!

To fix a run-on sentence, identify each complete thought or idea and break it into shorter sentences.

Kansas holds the record for having the largest ball of twine in the United States. Can you believe it weighs over 17,000 pounds? In fact, the giant ball is 40 feet in circumference, 11 feet tall, and made up of more than 1,100 miles of twine!

Rewrite each run-on sentence correctly. Remember to begin and end each sentence correctly. **Possible sentences:**

1. Did you know that the United States is the top meat-eating country in the world each person consumes about 260 pounds of meat each year beef is the most commonly eaten meat.
Did you know that the United States is the top meat-eating country in the world? Each person consumes about 260 pounds of meat each year. Beef is the most commonly eaten meat.

2. Have you ever noticed that Abraham Lincoln faces right on a penny he is the only president on a U.S. coin who does Sacagawea faces right on the new dollar coin, but she was not a president?
Have you ever noticed that Abraham Lincoln faces right on a penny? He is the only president on a U.S. coin who does. Sacagawea faces right on the new dollar coin, but she was not a president.

3. It would be fantastic to have a robot to do all my chores, help do my homework, and play games I really think the day will come unfortunately, it won't come soon enough for me.
It would be fantastic to have a robot to do all my chores, help do my homework, and play games. I really think the day will come. Unfortunately, it won't come soon enough for me.

page 53

Under the Big Top

The answer to a multiplication problem is called the product. The numbers being multiplied are called factors.

Multiply. Then use each product and the code to answer the riddles.

What happened to the human cannonball at the circus?

H (4×6) e (6×3) w (7×7) a (3×4) s (8×3) h (6×8) i (7×9) r (2×9) e (3×6) d (8×7)

a (6×2) n (8×9) d (7×3) f (9×9) i (8×6) r (9×7) e (3×6) d (7×8) o (7×6) n (9×8)

t (5×9) h (6×4) e (9×2) s (8×8) a (4×3) m (6×6) e (6×3) d (8×7) a (2×6) y! (5×5)

What happened to the kid who ran away with the circus?

H (3×8) e (2×9) h (4×6) a (3×8) d (8×7)

t (9×5) o (7×9) b (7×3) r (9×2) i (5×8) n (5×8) g (5×8)

i (6×8) t (5×9) b (3×9) a (2×6) c (5×3) k (9×6)

A = 12	H = 24	O = 42	V = 21
B = 28	I = 48	P = 16	W = 49
C = 15	J = 4	Q = 28	X = 1
D = 56	K = 54	R = 63	Y = 25
E = 18	L = 8	S = 64	Z = 2
F = 81	M = 36	T = 45	
G = 40	N = 72	U = 0	

page 54

A Long School Year

Have you ever accidentally left out words when you write? Whenever you write, it is always a good idea to proofread for words that may be missing. Here is an example of what to do when you want to add a missing word as you proofread.

e-mail
I got an ^from my friend last night.
met
We ^last summer when my family was in Japan.

Read the passage below about school in Japan. Twenty-one words are missing. Figure out what they are and add them to the sentences. Use the ^ symbol to show where each missing word belongs. Then write each missing word above the sentence. Hint: Every sentence has at least one missing word. **Answers may vary.**

you
How would like to go to school on Saturdays? If you lived in the ^of Japan, friend country
that's just where you'd be each Saturday morning. I have a ^who lives in Japan.
students days half
Yuichi explained that attend classes five and one-half ^a week. The day is on learn
Saturday. I was also surprised to that the Japanese school ^one of the longest year month
in the world—over 240 days. It begins in the ^of April. While we have over two summer vacation
months off each, students in Japan get their ^in late July and August. School begins Japan education
then ^again in fall and ends in March. The people of ^believe that a good is very age
important. Children are required to attend school from the age of six to the ^of schools students
fifteen. They have elementary and middle just like we do. Then most ^go on to high hard
^school for another three years. Yuichi says that students work very ^because the take
standards are so high. He and some of his friends even ^extra classes after college
school. They all want to get into a good ^someday.

Write several sentences on a sheet of paper about something that interests you. Rewrite the sentences on another sheet of paper, this time leaving out a key word in each one. Challenge someone at home to add the missing words. Then compare the two sets of sentences.

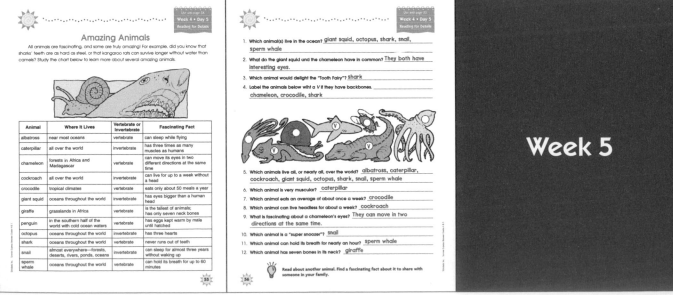

page 55

Amazing Animals

All animals are fascinating, and some are truly amazing! For example, did you know that sharks' teeth are as hard as steel, or that kangaroo rats can survive longer without water than camels? Study the chart below to learn more about several amazing animals.

Animal	Where It Lives	Vertebrate or Invertebrate	Fascinating Fact
albatross	near most oceans	vertebrate	can sleep while flying
caterpillar	all over the world	invertebrate	has three times as many muscles as humans
chameleon	forests in Africa and Madagascar	vertebrate	can move its eyes in two different directions at the same time
cockroach	all over the world	invertebrate	can live for up to a week without a head
crocodile	tropical climates	vertebrate	eats only about 50 meals a year
giant squid	oceans throughout the world	invertebrate	has eyes bigger than a human head
giraffe	grasslands in Africa	vertebrate	is the tallest of animals; has only seven neck bones
penguin	in the southern half of the world with cold ocean waters	vertebrate	has eggs kept warm by male until hatched
octopus	oceans throughout the world	invertebrate	has three hearts
shark	oceans throughout the world	vertebrate	never runs out of teeth
snail	almost everywhere—forests, deserts, rivers, ponds, oceans	invertebrate	can sleep for almost three years without waking up
sperm whale	oceans throughout the world	vertebrate	can hold its breath for up to 60 minutes

page 56

1. Which animal(s) live in the ocean? _giant squid, octopus, shark, snail, sperm whale_
2. What do the giant squid and the chameleon have in common? _They both have interesting eyes._
3. Which animal would delight the "Tooth Fairy"? _shark_
Label the animals below with a V if they have backbones.
chameleon, crocodile, shark

5. Which animals live all, or nearly all, over the world? _albatross, caterpillar, cockroach, giant squid, octopus, shark, snail, sperm whale_
6. Which animal is very muscular? _caterpillar_
7. Which animal eats an average of about once a week? _crocodile_
8. Which animal can live headless for about a week? _cockroach_
9. What is fascinating about a chameleon's eyes? _They can move in two directions at the same time._
10. Which animal is a "super snoozer"? _snail_
11. Which animal can hold its breath for nearly an hour? _sperm whale_
12. Which animal has seven bones in its neck? _giraffe_

Read about another animal. Find a fascinating fact about it to share with someone in your family.

Week 5

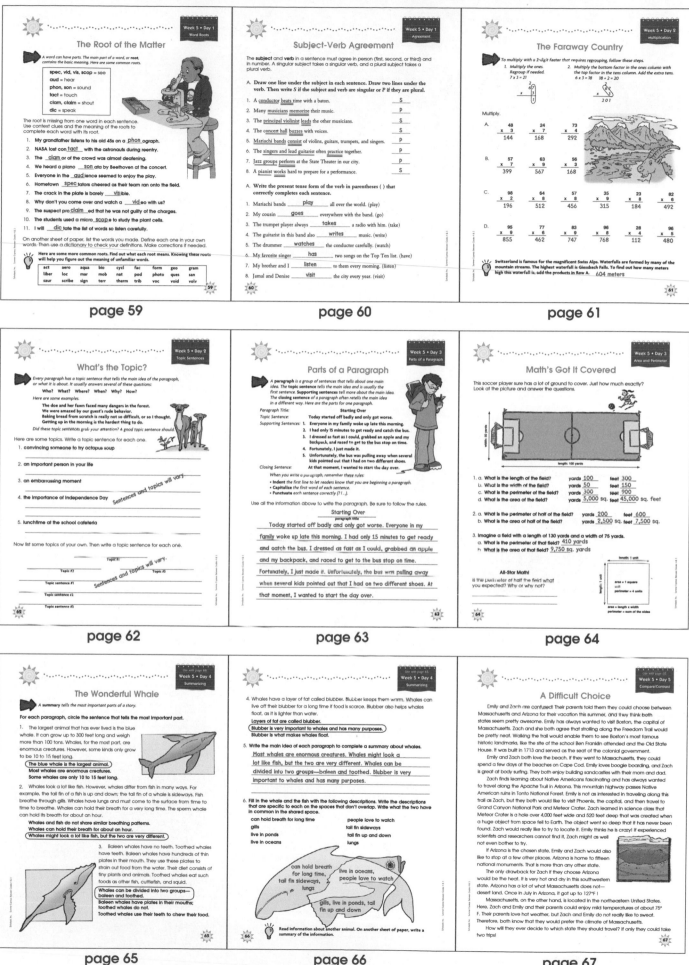

page 59

Week 5 • Day 1
Word Roots

The Root of the Matter

A word can have parts. The main part of a word, or **root**, *contains the basic meaning. Here are some common roots.*

spec, vid, vis, scop = see
aud = hear
phon, son = sound
tact = touch
clam, claim = shout
dic = speak

The root is missing from one word in each sentence. Use context clues and the meaning of the roots to complete each word with its root.

1. My grandfather listens to his old 45s on a phon ograph.
2. NASA lost con tact with the astronauts during reentry.
3. The clam or of the crowd was almost deafening.
4. We heard a piano son ata by Beethoven at the concert.
5. Everyone in the aud ience seemed to enjoy the play.
6. Hometown spec tators cheered as their team ran onto the field.
7. The crack in the plate is barely vis ible.
8. Why don't you come over and watch a vid eo with us?
9. The suspect pro claim ed that he was not guilty of the charges.
10. The students used a micro scop e to study the plant cells.
11. I will dic tate the list of words so listen carefully.

On another sheet of paper, list the words you made. Define each one in your own words. Then use a dictionary to check your definitions. Make corrections if needed.

Here are some more common roots. Find out what each root means. Knowing these roots will help you figure out the meaning of unfamiliar words.

act	aero	aqua	bio	cycl	fac	form	geo	gram
liber	loc	mar	mob	nat	pod	photo	ques	san
saur	scribe	sign	terr	therm	trib	voc	void	volv

59

page 60

Week 5 • Day 1
Agreement

Subject-Verb Agreement

The **subject** and **verb** in a sentence must agree in person (first, second, or third) and in number. A singular subject takes a singular verb, and a plural subject takes a plural verb.

A. **Draw one line under the subject in each sentence. Draw two lines under the verb. Then write *S* if the subject and verb are singular or *P* if they are plural.**

1. A conductor beats time with a baton. S
2. Many musicians memorize their music. P
3. The principal violinist leads the other musicians. S
4. The concert hall buzzes with voices. S
5. Mariachi bands consist of violins, guitars, trumpets, and singers. P
6. The singers and lead guitarist often practice together. P
7. Jazz groups perform at the State Theater in our city. P
8. A pianist works hard to prepare for a performance. S

A. **Write the present tense form of the verb in parentheses ( ) that correctly completes each sentence.**

1. Mariachi bands play all over the world. (play)
2. My cousin goes everywhere with the band. (go)
3. The trumpet player always takes a radio with him. (take)
4. The guitarist in this band also writes music. (write)
5. The drummer watches the conductor carefully. (watch)
6. My favorite singer has two songs on the Top Ten list. (have)
7. My brother and I listen to them every morning. (listen)
8. Jamal and Denise visit the city every year. (visit)

60

page 61

Week 5 • Day 2
Multiplication

The Faraway Country

To multiply with a 2-digit factor that requires regrouping, follow these steps.

1. *Multiply the ones. Regroup if needed.* $7 \times 3 = 21$
2. *Multiply the bottom factor in the ones column with the top factor in the tens column. Add the extra tens.* $6 \times 3 = 18$ $18 + 2 = 20$

$$\begin{array}{r} {}^{2}\\ 67\\ \times\ 3\\ \hline 1 \end{array} \qquad \begin{array}{r} {}^{2}\\ 67\\ \times\ 3\\ \hline 201 \end{array}$$

Multiply.

A.	48 × 3 = 144	24 × 7 = 168	73 × 4 = 292			
B.	57 × 7 = 399	63 × 9 = 567	56 × 3 = 168			
C.	98 × 2 = 196	64 × 8 = 512	57 × 8 = 456	35 × 9 = 315	23 × 8 = 184	82 × 6 = 492
D.	95 × 9 = 855	77 × 6 = 462	83 × 9 = 747	96 × 8 = 768	28 × 4 = 112	96 × 5 = 480

Switzerland is famous for the magnificent Swiss Alps. Waterfalls are formed by many of the mountain streams. The highest waterfall is Giessbach Falls. To find out how many meters high this waterfall is, add the products in Row A. 604 meters

61

page 62

Week 5 • Day 2
Topic Sentences

What's the Topic?

Every paragraph has a topic sentence that tells the main idea of the paragraph, or what it is about. It usually answers several of these questions:

Who? What? Where? When? Why? How?

Here are some examples.

The doe and her fawn faced many dangers in the forest.
We were amazed by our guest's rude behavior.
Baking bread from scratch is really not so difficult, or so I thought.
Getting up in the morning is the hardest thing to do.

Did these topic sentences grab your attention? A good topic sentence should.

Here are some topics. Write a topic sentence for each one.

1. convincing someone to try octopus soup
2. an important person in your life
3. an embarrassing moment
4. the importance of Independence Day
5. lunchtime at the school cafeteria

Sentences and topics will vary.

Now list some topics of your own. Then write a topic sentence for each one.

Topic #1
Topic #2
Topic #3
Topic sentence #1
Topic sentence #2
Topic sentence #3

Sentences and topics will vary.

62

page 63

Week 5 • Day 3
Parts of a Paragraph

Parts of a Paragraph

A **paragraph** *is a group of sentences that tells about one main idea. The* **topic sentence** *tells the main idea and is usually the first sentence.* **Supporting sentences** *tell more about the main idea. The* **closing sentence** *of a paragraph often retells the main idea in a different way. Here are the parts for one paragraph.*

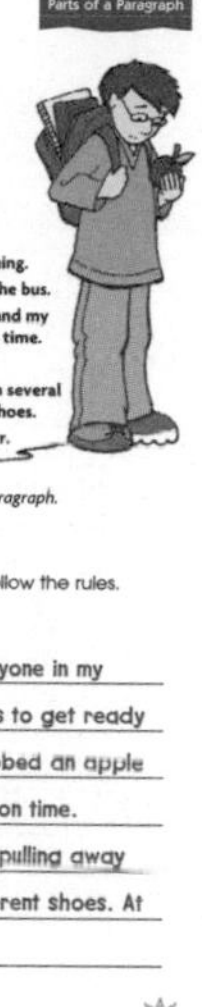

Paragraph Title: **Starting Over**
Topic Sentence: **Today started off badly and only got worse.**
Supporting Sentences:
1. **Everyone in my family woke up late this morning.**
2. **I had only 15 minutes to get ready and catch the bus.**
3. **I dressed as fast as I could, grabbed an apple and my backpack, and raced to get to the bus stop on time.**
4. **Fortunately, I just made it.**
5. **Unfortunately, the bus was pulling away when several kids pointed out that I had on two different shoes.**

Closing Sentence: **At that moment, I wanted to start the day over.**

When you write a paragraph, remember these rules:

- **Indent** *the first line to let readers know that you are beginning a paragraph.*
- **Capitalize** *the first word of each sentence.*
- **Punctuate** *each sentence correctly (? ! . ,).*

Use all the information above to write the paragraph. Be sure to follow the rules.

Starting Over
paragraph title

Today started off badly and only got worse. Everyone in my family woke up late this morning. I had only 15 minutes to get ready and catch the bus. I dressed as fast as I could, grabbed an apple and my backpack, and raced to get to the bus stop on time. Fortunately, I just made it. Unfortunately, the bus was pulling away when several kids pointed out that I had on two different shoes. At that moment, I wanted to start the day over.

62

page 64

Week 5 • Day 3
Area and Perimeter

Math's Got It Covered

This soccer player sure has a lot of ground to cover. Just how much exactly? Look at the picture and answer the questions.

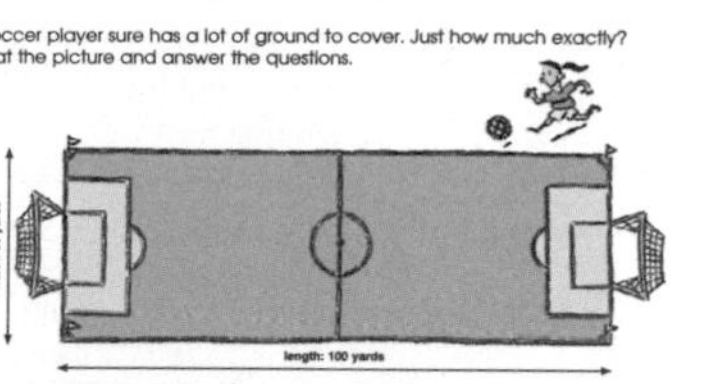

width: 50 yards
length: 100 yards

1. a. What is the length of the field? yards 100 feet 300
   b. What is the width of the field? yards 50 feet 150
   c. What is the perimeter of the field? yards 300 feet 900
   d. What is the area of the field? yards 5,000 sq. feet 45,000 sq. feet
2. a. What is the perimeter of half of the field? yards 200 feet 600
   b. What is the area of half of the field? yards 2,500 sq. feet 7,500 sq.
3. Imagine a field with a length of 130 yards and a width of 75 yards.
   a. What is the perimeter of that field? 410 yards
   b. What is the area of that field? 9,750 sq. yards

All-Star Math!

Is the perimeter of half the field what you expected? Why or why not?

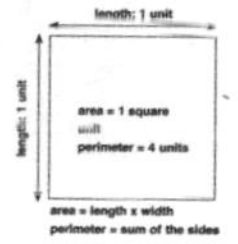

length: 1 unit
length: 1 unit
area = 1 square unit
perimeter = 4 units

area = length x width
perimeter = sum of the sides

64

page 65

Use with page 66.
Week 5 • Day 4
Summarizing

The Wonderful Whale

A summary *tells the most important parts of a story.*

For each paragraph, circle the sentence that tells the most important part.

1. The largest animal that has ever lived is the blue whale. It can grow up to 300 feet long and weigh more than 100 tons. Whales, for the most part, are enormous creatures. However, some kinds only grow to be 10 to 15 feet long.

The blue whale is the largest animal. (circled)
Most whales are enormous creatures.
Some whales are only 10 to 15 feet long.

2. Whales look a lot like fish. However, whales differ from fish in many ways. For example, the tail fin of a fish is up and down; the tail fin of a whale is sideways. Fish breathe through gills. Whales have lungs and must come to the surface from time to time to breathe. Whales can hold their breath for a very long time. The sperm whale can hold its breath for about an hour.

Whales and fish do not share similar breathing patterns.
Whales can hold their breath for about an hour.
Whales might look a lot like fish, but the two are very different. (circled)

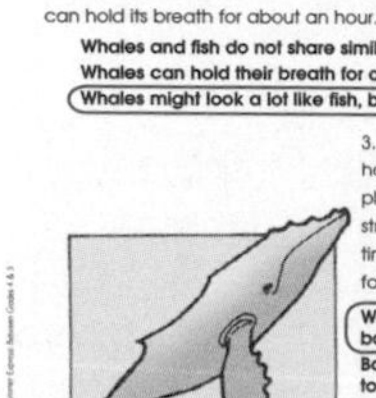

3. Baleen whales have no teeth. Toothed whales have teeth. Baleen whales have hundreds of thin plates in their mouth. They use these plates to strain out food from the water. Their diet consists of tiny plants and animals. Toothed whales eat such foods as other fish, cuttlefish, and squid.

Whales can be divided into two groups—baleen and toothed. (circled)
Baleen whales have plates in their mouths; toothed whales do not.
Toothed whales use their teeth to chew their food.

65

page 66

Use with page 65.
Week 5 • Day 4
Summarizing

4. Whales have a layer of fat called blubber. Blubber keeps them warm. Whales can live off their blubber for a long time if food is scarce. Blubber also helps whales float, as it is lighter than water.

Layers of fat are called blubber.
Blubber is very important to whales and has many purposes. (circled)
Blubber is what makes whales float.

5. **Write the main idea of each paragraph to complete a summary about whales.**

Most whales are enormous creatures. Whales might look a lot like fish, but the two are very different. Whales can be divided into two groups—baleen and toothed. Blubber is very important to whales and has many purposes.

6. **Fill in the whale and the fish with the following descriptions. Write the descriptions that are specific to each on the spaces that don't overlap. Write what the two have in common in the shared space.**

can hold breath for long time	people love to watch
gills	tail fin sideways
live in ponds	tail fin up and down
live in oceans	lungs

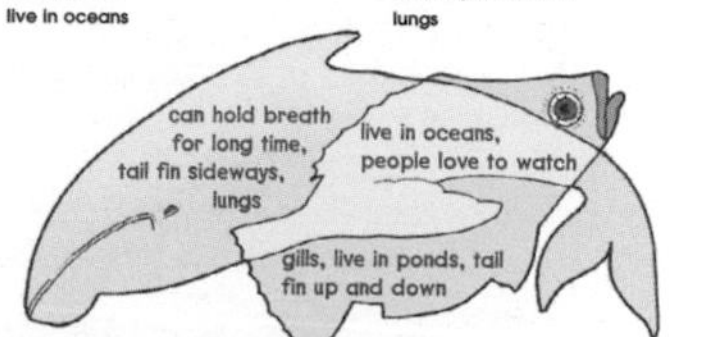

can hold breath for long time, tail fin sideways, lungs
live in oceans, people love to watch
gills, live in ponds, tail fin up and down

Read information about another animal. On another sheet of paper, write a summary of the information.

66

page 67

Use with page 68.
Week 5 • Day 5
Compare/Contrast

A Difficult Choice

Emily and Zach are confused! Their parents told them they could choose between Massachusetts and Arizona for their vacation this summer, and they think both states seem pretty awesome. Emily has always wanted to visit Boston, the capital of Massachusetts. Zach and she both agree that strolling along the Freedom Trail would be pretty neat. Walking the trail would enable them to see Boston's most famous historic landmarks, like the site of the school Ben Franklin attended and the Old State House. It was built in 1713 and served as the seat of the colonial government.

Emily and Zach both love the beach. If they went to Massachusetts, they could spend a few days at the beaches on Cape Cod. Emily loves boogie boarding, and Zach is great at body surfing. They both enjoy building sandcastles with their mom and dad.

Zach finds learning about Native Americans fascinating and has always wanted to travel along the Apache Trail in Arizona. This mountain highway passes Native American ruins in Tonto National Forest. Emily is not as interested in traveling along this trail as Zach, but they both would like to visit Phoenix, the capital, and then travel to Grand Canyon National Park and Meteor Crater. Zach learned in science class that Meteor Crater is a hole over 4,000 feet wide and 520 feet deep that was created when a huge object from space fell to Earth. The object went so deep that it has never been found. Zach would really like to try to locate it. Emily thinks he is crazy! If experienced scientists and researchers cannot find it, Zach might as well not even bother to try.

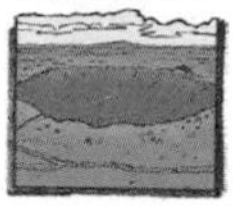

If Arizona is the chosen state, Emily and Zach would also like to stop at a few other places. Arizona is home to fifteen national monuments. That is more than any other state.

The only drawback for Zach if they choose Arizona would be the heat. It is very hot and dry in this southwestern state. Arizona has a lot of what Massachusetts does not—desert land. Once in July in Arizona, it got up to 127°F !

Massachusetts, on the other hand, is located in the northeastern United States. Here, Zach and Emily and their parents could enjoy mild temperatures of about 75° F. Their parents love hot weather, but Zach and Emily do not really like to sweat. Therefore, both know that they would prefer the climate of Massachusetts.

How will they ever decide to which state they should travel? If only they could take two trips!

67

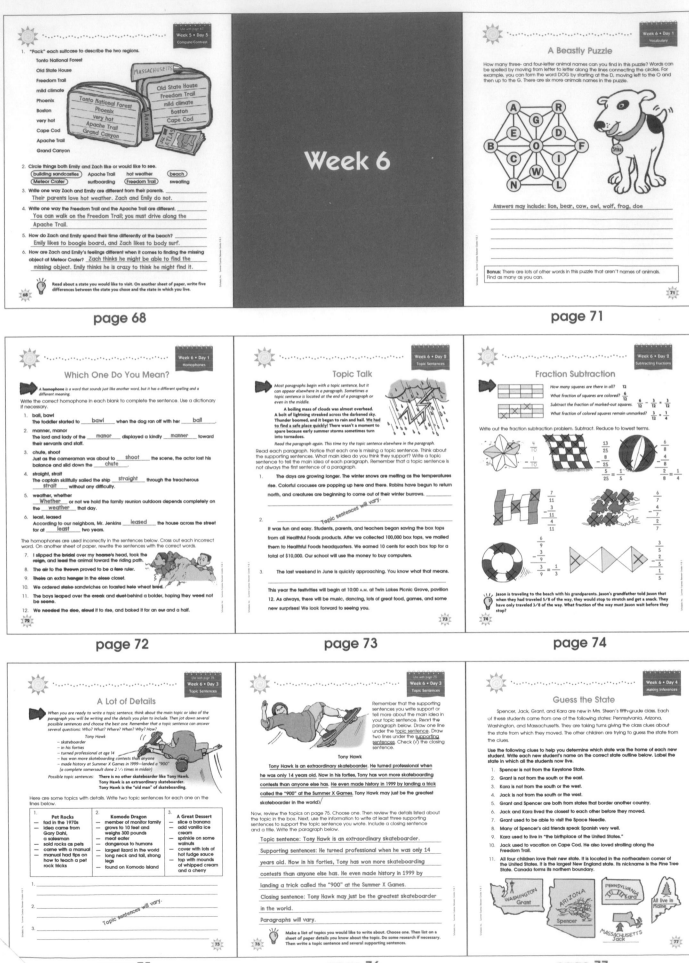

page 68

1. "Pack" each suitcase to describe the two regions.

Tonto National Forest
Old State House
Freedom Trail
mild climate
Phoenix
Boston
very hot
Cape Cod
Apache Trail
Grand Canyon

MASSACHUSETTS: Old State House, Freedom Trail, mild climate, Boston, Cape Cod
ARIZONA: Tonto National Forest, Phoenix, very hot, Apache Trail, Grand Canyon

2. Circle things both Emily and Zach like or would like to see.
(building sandcastles) Apache Trail hot weather (beach)
(Meteor Crater) surfboarding (Freedom Trail) sweating

3. Write one way Zach and Emily are different from their parents.
Their parents love hot weather. Zach and Emily do not.

4. Write one way the Freedom Trail and the Apache Trail are different.
You can walk on the Freedom Trail; you must drive along the Apache Trail.

5. How do Zach and Emily spend their time differently at the beach?
Emily likes to boogie board, and Zach likes to body surf.

6. How are Zach and Emily's feelings different when it comes to finding the missing object at Meteor Crater? Zach thinks he might be able to find the missing object. Emily thinks he is crazy to think he might find it.

Read about a state you would like to visit. On another sheet of paper, write five differences between the state you chose and the state in which you live.

Week 6

---

page 71

A Beastly Puzzle

How many three- and four-letter animal names can you find in this puzzle? Words can be spelled by moving from letter to letter along the lines connecting the circles. For example, you can form the word DOG by starting at the D, moving left to the O and then up to the G. There are six more animals names in the puzzle.

Answers may include: lion, bear, cow, owl, wolf, frog, doe

Bonus: There are lots of other words in this puzzle that aren't names of animals. Find as many as you can.

---

page 72

Which One Do You Mean?

A homophone is a word that sounds just like another word, but it has a different spelling and a different meaning.

Write the correct homophone in each blank to complete the sentence. Use a dictionary if necessary.

1. ball, bawl
The toddler started to __bawl__ when the dog ran off with her __ball__.

2. manor, manner
The lord and lady of the __manor__ displayed a kindly __manner__ toward their servants and staff.

3. chute, shoot
Just as the cameraman was about to __shoot__ the scene, the actor lost his balance and slid down the __chute__.

4. straight, strait
The captain skillfully sailed the ship __straight__ through the treacherous __strait__ without any difficulty.

5. weather, whether
__Whether__ or not we hold the family reunion outdoors depends completely on the __weather__ that day.

6. least, leased
According to our neighbors, Mr. Jenkins __leased__ the house across the street for at __least__ two years.

The homophones are used incorrectly in the sentences below. Cross out each incorrect word. On another sheet of paper, rewrite the sentences with the correct words.

7. I slipped the bridal over my hoarse's head, took the rein, and leed the animal toward the riding path.
8. The air to the thrown proved to be a fare ruler.
9. Thair an extra hanger in the close closet.
10. We ordered stake sandwiches on toasted hole wheat bred.
11. The boys leaped over the creek and duct behind a bolder, hoping they weed not be seene.
12. We needed the doe, aloud it to rise, and baked it for an our and a half.

---

page 73

Topic Talk

Most paragraphs begin with a topic sentence, but it can appear elsewhere in a paragraph. Sometimes a topic sentence is located at the end of a paragraph or even in the middle.

A boiling mass of clouds was almost overhead. A bolt of lightning streaked across the darkened sky. Thunder boomed, and it began to rain and hail. We had to find a safe place quickly! There wasn't a moment to spare because early summer storms sometimes turn into tornadoes.

Read the paragraph again. This time try the topic sentence elsewhere in the paragraph.

Read each paragraph. Notice that each one is missing a topic sentence. Think about the supporting sentences. What main idea do you think they support? Write a topic sentence to tell the main idea of each paragraph. Remember that a topic sentence is not always the first sentence of a paragraph.

1. _____
The days are growing longer. The winter snows are melting as the temperatures rise. Colorful crocuses are popping up here and there. Robins have begun to return north, and creatures are beginning to come out of their winter burrows.

2. _____
It was fun and easy. Students, parents, and teachers began saving the box tops from all Healthful Foods products. After we collected 100,000 box tops, we mailed them to Healthful Foods headquarters. We earned 10 cents for each box top for a total of $10,000. Our school will use the money to buy computers.

3. _____
The last weekend in June is quickly approaching. You know what that means. This year the festivities will begin at 10:00 A.M. at Twin Lakes Picnic Grove, pavilion 12. As always, there will be music, dancing, lots of great food, games, and some new surprises! We look forward to seeing you.

Topic sentences will vary.

---

page 74

Fraction Subtraction

How many squares are there in all? 12
What fraction of squares are colored? $\frac{6}{12}$
Subtract the fraction of marked-out squares. $\frac{6}{12} - \frac{3}{12} = \frac{3}{12}$
What fraction of colored squares remain unmarked? $\frac{3}{12} = \frac{1}{4}$

Write out the fraction subtraction problem. Subtract. Reduce to lowest terms.

$\frac{4}{10} - \frac{1}{10}$

$\frac{13}{25} - \frac{8}{25} = \frac{5}{25} = \frac{1}{5}$

$\frac{6}{8} - \frac{2}{8} = \frac{4}{8} = \frac{1}{2}$

$\frac{7}{11} - \frac{3}{11} = \frac{4}{11}$

$\frac{6}{7} - \frac{2}{7} = \frac{4}{7}$

$\frac{6}{9} - \frac{3}{9} = \frac{3}{9} = \frac{1}{3}$

$\frac{5}{5} - \frac{3}{5} = \frac{2}{5}$

Jason is traveling to the beach with his grandparents. Jason's grandfather told Jason that when they had traveled 5/8 of the way, they would stop to stretch and get a snack. They have only traveled 3/8 of the way. What fraction of the way must Jason wait before they stop?

---

page 75

A Lot of Details

When you are ready to write a topic sentence, think about the main topic or idea of the paragraph you will be writing and the details you plan to include. Then jot down several possible sentences and choose the best one. Remember that a topic sentence can answer several questions: Who? What? Where? When? Why? How?

Tony Hawk
– skateboarder
– in his forties
– turned professional at age 14
– has won more skateboarding contests than anyone
– made history at Summer X Games in 1999—landed a "900" (a complete somersault done 2 ½ times in midair)

Possible topic sentences: There is no other skateboarder like Tony Hawk.
Tony Hawk is an extraordinary skateboarder.
Tony Hawk is the "old man" of skateboarding.

Here are some topics with details. Write two topic sentences for each one on the lines below.

1. Pet Rocks	2. Komodo Dragon	3. A Great Dessert
– fad in the 1970s	– member of monitor family	– slice a banana
– idea came from Gary Dahl, a salesman	– grows to 10 feet and weighs 300 pounds	– add vanilla ice cream
– sold rocks as pets	– meat eater	– sprinkle on some walnuts
– came with a manual	– dangerous to humans	– cover with lots of hot fudge sauce
– manual had tips on how to teach a pet rock tricks	– largest lizard in the world	– top with mounds of whipped cream and a cherry
	– long neck and tail, strong legs	
	– found on Komodo Island	

1. _____
2. _____
3. _____

Topic sentences will vary.

---

page 76

Remember that the supporting sentences you write support or tell more about the main idea in your topic sentence. Reread the paragraph below. Draw one line under the topic sentence. Draw two lines under the supporting sentences. Check (✓) the closing sentence.

Tony Hawk
Tony Hawk is an extraordinary skateboarder. He turned professional when he was only 14 years old. Now in his forties, Tony has won more skateboarding contests than anyone else has. He even made history in 1999 by landing a trick called the "900" at the Summer X Games. Tony Hawk may just be the greatest skateboarder in the world.✓

Now, review the topics on page 75. Choose one. Then review the details listed about the topic in the box. Next, use the information to write at least three supporting sentences to support the topic sentence you wrote. Include a closing sentence and a title. Write the paragraph below.

Topic sentence: Tony Hawk is an extraordinary skateboarder.

Supporting sentences: He turned professional when he was only 14 years old. Now in his forties, Tony has won more skateboarding contests than anyone else has. He even made history in 1999 by landing a trick called the "900" at the Summer X Games.

Closing sentence: Tony Hawk may just be the greatest skateboarder in the world.

Paragraphs will vary.

Make a list of topics you would like to write about. Choose one. Then list on a sheet of paper details you know about the topic. Do some research if necessary. Then write a topic sentence and several supporting sentences.

---

page 77

Guess the State

Spencer, Jack, Grant, and Kara are new in Mrs. Steen's fifth-grade class. Each of these students came from one of the following states: Pennsylvania, Arizona, Washington, and Massachusetts. They are taking turns giving the class clues about the state from which they moved. The other children are trying to guess the state from the clues.

Use the following clues to help you determine which state was the home of each new student. Write each new student's name on the correct state outline below. Label the state in which all the students now live.

1. Spencer is not from the Keystone State.
2. Grant is not from the south or the east.
3. Kara is not from the south or the west.
4. Jack is not from the south or the west.
5. Grant and Spencer are both from states that border another country.
6. Jack and Kara lived the closest to each other before they moved.
7. Grant used to be able to visit the Space Needle.
8. Many of Spencer's old friends speak Spanish very well.
9. Kara used to live in "the birthplace of the United States."
10. Jack used to vacation on Cape Cod. He also loved strolling along the Freedom Trail.
11. All four children love their new state. It is located in the northeastern corner of the United States. It is the largest New England state. Its nickname is the Pine Tree State. Canada forms its northern boundary.

WASHINGTON: Grant
ARIZONA: Spencer
PENNSYLVANIA: Kara
MASSACHUSETTS: Jack
All live in Maine

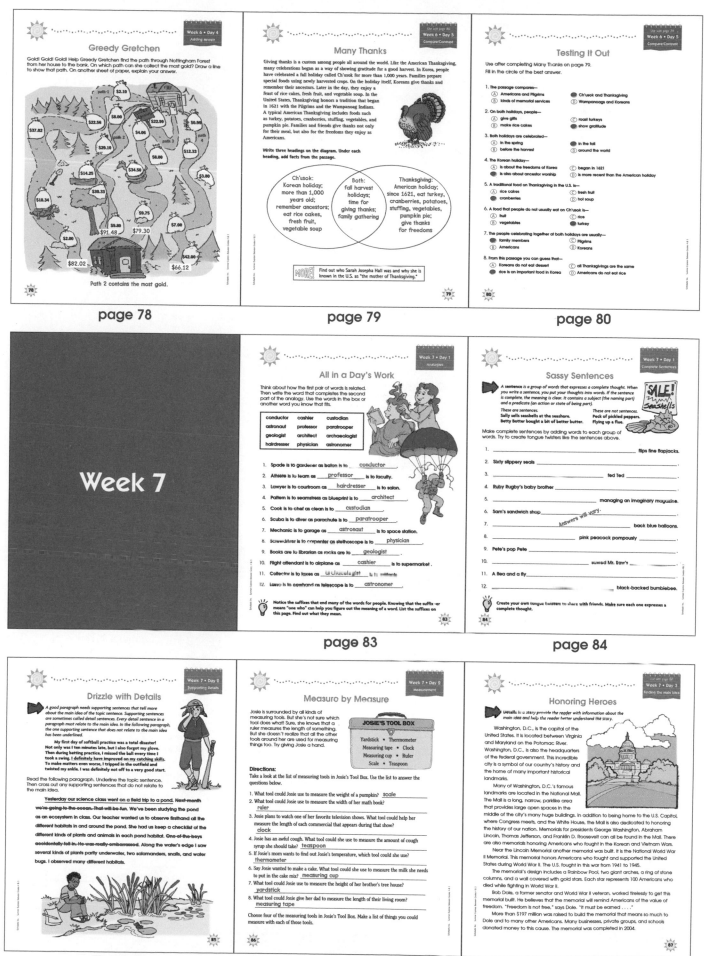

page 78

Greedy Gretchen

Gold! Gold! Gold! Help Greedy Gretchen find the path through Nottingham Forest from her house to the bank. On which path can she collect the most gold? Draw a line to show that path. On another sheet of paper, explain your answer.

Path 2 contains the most gold.

Week 6 • Day 4 — Adding Money

page 79

Many Thanks

Giving thanks is a custom among people all around the world. Like the American Thanksgiving, many celebrations began as a way of showing gratitude for a good harvest. In Korea, people have celebrated a fall holiday called Ch'usok for more than 1,000 years. Families prepare special foods using newly harvested crops. On the holiday itself, Koreans give thanks and remember their ancestors. Later in the day, they enjoy a feast of rice cakes, fresh fruit, and vegetable soup. In the United States, Thanksgiving honors a tradition that began in 1621 with the Pilgrims and the Wampanoag Indians. A typical American Thanksgiving includes foods such as turkey, potatoes, cranberries, stuffing, vegetables, and pumpkin pie. Families and friends give thanks not only for their meal, but also for the freedoms they enjoy as Americans.

Write three headings on the diagram. Under each heading, add facts from the passage.

Ch'usok: Korean holiday; more than 1,000 years old; remember ancestors; eat rice cakes, fresh fruit, vegetable soup

Both: fall harvest holidays; time for giving thanks; family gathering

Thanksgiving: American holiday; since 1621, eat turkey, cranberries, potatoes, stuffing, vegetables, pumpkin pie; give thanks for freedoms

MORE! Find out who Sarah Josepha Hall was and why she is known in the U.S. as "the mother of Thanksgiving."

Week 6 • Day 5 — Compare/Contrast

page 80

Testing It Out

Use after completing Many Thanks on page 79.
Fill in the circle of the best answer.

1. The passage compares—
   - (A) Americans and Pilgrims
   - (B) kinds of memorial services
   - ● Ch'usok and Thanksgiving
   - (D) Wampanoags and Koreans

2. On both holidays, people—
   - (A) give gifts
   - (B) make rice cakes
   - (C) roast turkeys
   - ● show gratitude

3. Both holidays are celebrated—
   - (A) in the spring
   - (B) before the harvest
   - ● in the fall
   - (D) around the world

4. The Korean holiday—
   - (A) is about the freedoms of Korea
   - ● is also about ancestor worship
   - (C) began in 1621
   - (D) is more recent than the American holiday

5. A traditional food on Thanksgiving in the U.S. is—
   - (A) rice cakes
   - ● cranberries
   - (C) fresh fruit
   - (D) hot soup

6. A food that people do not usually eat on Ch'usok is—
   - (A) fruit
   - (B) vegetables
   - (C) rice
   - ● turkey

7. The people celebrating together at both holidays are usually—
   - ● family members
   - (B) Americans
   - (C) Pilgrims
   - (D) Koreans

8. From this passage you can guess that—
   - (A) Koreans do not eat dessert
   - ● rice is an important food in Korea
   - (C) all Thanksgivings are the same
   - (D) Americans do not eat rice

Week 6 • Day 5 — Compare/Contrast

Week 7

page 83

All in a Day's Work

Think about how the first pair of words is related. Then write the word that completes the second part of the analogy. Use the words in the box or another word you know that fits.

conductor	cashier	custodian
astronaut	professor	paratrooper
geologist	architect	archaeologist
hairdresser	physician	astronomer

1. Spade is to gardener as baton is to ___conductor___
2. Athlete is to team as ___professor___ is to faculty.
3. Lawyer is to courtroom as ___hairdresser___ is to salon.
4. Pattern is to seamstress as blueprint is to ___architect___
5. Cook is to chef as clean is to ___custodian___
6. Scuba is to diver as parachute is to ___paratrooper___
7. Mechanic is to garage as ___astronaut___ is to space station.
8. Screwdriver is to carpenter as stethoscope is to ___physician___
9. Books are to librarian as rocks are to ___geologist___
10. Flight attendant is to airplane as ___cashier___ is to supermarket.
11. Collector is to taxes as archaeologist is to artifacts.
12. Lasso is to cowhand as telescope is to ___astronomer___

Notice the suffixes that end many of the words for people. Knowing that the suffix -er means "one who" can help you figure out the meaning of a word. List the suffixes on this page. Find out what they mean.

Week 7 • Day 1 — Analogies

page 84

Sassy Sentences

A sentence is a group of words that expresses a complete thought. When you write a sentence, you put your thoughts into words. If the sentence is complete, the meaning is clear. It contains a subject (the naming part) and a predicate (an action or state of being part).

These are sentences.
Sally sells seashells at the seashore.
Betty Botter bought a bit of better butter.

These are not sentences.
Peck of pickled peppers.
Flying up a flue.

Make complete sentences by adding words to each group of words. Try to create tongue twisters like the sentences above.

1. ___ flips fine flapjacks.
2. Sixty slippery seals ___
3. ___ fed Ted
4. Ruby Rugby's baby brother ___
5. ___ managing an imaginary magazine.
6. Sam's sandwich shop ___
7. ___ back blue balloons.
8. ___ pink peacock pompously
9. Pete's pop Pete ___
10. ___ sawed Mr. Saw's ___
11. A flea and a fly ___
12. ___ black-backed bumblebee.

Answers will vary.

Create your own tongue twisters to share with friends. Make sure each one expresses a complete thought.

Week 7 • Day 1 — Complete Sentences

page 85

Drizzle with Details

A good paragraph needs supporting sentences that tell more about the main idea of the topic sentence. Supporting sentences are sometimes called detail sentences. Every detail sentence in a paragraph must relate to the main idea. In the following paragraph, the one supporting sentence that does not relate to the main idea has been underlined.

My first day of softball practice was a total disaster! Not only was I ten minutes late, but I also forgot my glove. Then during batting practice, I missed the ball every time I took a swing. I definitely have improved on my catching skills. To make matters even worse, I tripped in the outfield and twisted my ankle. I was definitely not off to a very good start.

Read the following paragraph. Underline the topic sentence. Then cross out any supporting sentences that do not relate to the main idea.

Yesterday our science class went on a field trip to a pond. ~~Next month we're going to the ocean. That will be fun.~~ We've been studying the pond as an ecosystem in class. Our teacher wanted us to observe firsthand all the different habitats in and around the pond. She had us keep a checklist of the different kinds of plants and animals in each pond habitat. ~~One of the boys accidentally fell in. He was really embarrassed.~~ Along the water's edge I saw several kinds of plants partly underwater, two salamanders, snails, and water bugs. I observed many different habitats.

Week 7 • Day 2 — Supporting Details

page 86

Measure by Measure

Josie is surrounded by all kinds of measuring tools. But she's not sure which tool does what! Sure, she knows that a ruler measures the length of something. But she doesn't realize that all the other tools around her are used for measuring things too. Try giving Josie a hand.

JOSIE'S TOOL BOX
Yardstick • Thermometer
Measuring tape • Clock
Measuring cup • Ruler
Scale • Teaspoon

Directions:
Take a look at the list of measuring tools in Josie's Tool Box. Use the list to answer the questions below.

1. What tool could Josie use to measure the weight of a pumpkin? ___scale___
2. What tool could Josie use to measure the width of her math book? ___ruler___
3. Josie plans to watch one of her favorite television shows. What tool could help her measure the length of each commercial that appears during that show? ___clock___
4. Josie has an awful cough. What tool could she use to measure the amount of cough syrup she should take? ___teaspoon___
5. If Josie's mom wants to find out Josie's temperature, which tool could she use? ___thermometer___
6. Say Josie wanted to make a cake. What tool could she use to measure the milk she needs to put in the cake mix? ___measuring cup___
7. What tool could Josie use to measure the height of her brother's tree house? ___yardstick___
8. What tool could Josie give her dad to measure the length of their living room? ___measuring tape___

Choose four of the measuring tools in Josie's Tool Box. Make a list of things you could measure with each of those tools.

Week 7 • Day 2 — Measurement

page 87

Honoring Heroes

Details in a story provide the reader with information about the main idea and help the reader better understand the story.

Washington, D.C. is the capital of the United States. It is located between Virginia and Maryland on the Potomac River. Washington, D.C., is also the headquarters of the federal government. This incredible city is a symbol of our country's history and the home of many important historical landmarks.

Many of Washington, D.C.'s famous landmarks are located in the National Mall. The Mall is a long, narrow, parklike area that provides large open spaces in the middle of the city's many huge buildings. In addition to being home to the U.S. Capitol, where Congress meets, and the White House, the Mall is also dedicated to honoring the history of our nation. Memorials for presidents George Washington, Abraham Lincoln, Thomas Jefferson, and Franklin D. Roosevelt can be found in the Mall. There are also memorials honoring Americans who fought in the Korean and Vietnam wars.

Near the Lincoln Memorial another memorial was built. It is the National World War II Memorial. This memorial honors Americans who fought and supported the United States during World War II. The U.S. fought in this war from 1941 to 1945.

The memorial's design includes a Rainbow Pool, two giant arches, a ring of stone columns, and a wall covered with gold stars. Each star represents 100 Americans who died while fighting in World War II.

Bob Dole, a former senator and World War II veteran, worked tirelessly to get this memorial built. He believes that the memorial will remind Americans of the value of freedom. "Freedom is not free," says Dole. "It must be earned . . . ."

More than $197 million was raised to build the memorial that means so much to Dole and to many other Americans. Many businesses, private groups, and schools donated money to this cause. The memorial was completed in 2004.

Week 7 • Day 3 — Finding the Main Idea

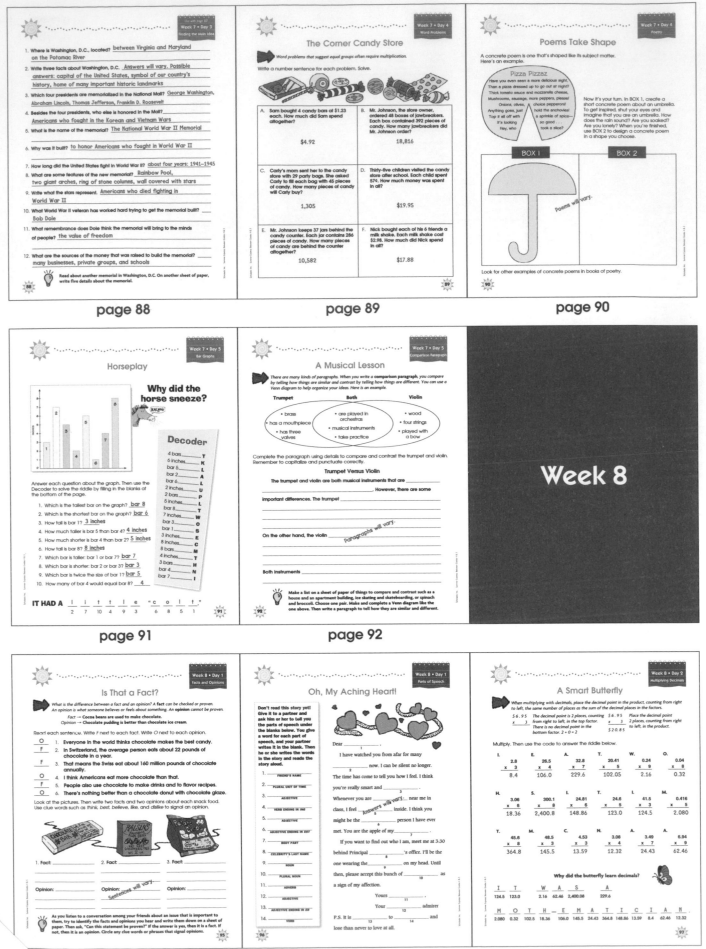

page 88

1. Where is Washington, D.C., located? between Virginia and Maryland on the Potomac River

2. Write three facts about Washington, D.C. Answers will vary. Possible answers: capital of the United States, symbol of our country's history, home of many important historic landmarks

3. Which four presidents are memorialized in the National Mall? George Washington, Abraham Lincoln, Thomas Jefferson, Franklin D. Roosevelt

4. Besides the four presidents, who else is honored in the Mall? Americans who fought in the Korean and Vietnam Wars

5. What is the name of the memorial? The National World War II Memorial

6. Why was it built? to honor Americans who fought in World War II

7. How long did the United States fight in World War II? about four years: 1941–1945

8. What are some features of the new memorial? Rainbow Pool, two giant arches, ring of stone columns, wall covered with stars

9. Write what the stars represent. Americans who died fighting in World War II

10. What World War II veteran has worked hard trying to get the memorial built? Bob Dole

11. What remembrance does Dole think the memorial will bring to the minds of people? the value of freedom

12. What are the sources of the money that was raised to build the memorial? many businesses, private groups, and schools

Read about another memorial in Washington, D.C. On another sheet of paper, write five details about the memorial.

page 89

The Corner Candy Store

Word problems that suggest equal groups often require multiplication.

Write a number sentence for each problem. Solve.

A. Sam bought 4 candy bars at $1.23 each. How much did Sam spend altogether?
$4.92

B. Mr. Johnson, the store owner, ordered 48 boxes of jawbreakers. Each box contained 392 pieces of candy. How many jawbreakers did Mr. Johnson order?
18,816

C. Carly's mom sent her to the candy store with 29 party bags. She asked Carly to fill each bag with 45 pieces of candy. How many pieces of candy will Carly buy?
1,305

D. Thirty-five children visited the candy store after school. Each child spent 57¢. How much money was spent in all?
$19.95

E. Mr. Johnson keeps 37 jars behind the candy counter. Each jar contains 286 pieces of candy. How many pieces of candy are behind the counter altogether?
10,582

F. Nick bought each of his 6 friends a milk shake. Each milk shake cost $2.98. How much did Nick spend in all?
$17.88

page 90

Poems Take Shape

A concrete poem is one that's shaped like its subject matter. Here's an example.

Pizza Pizzaz
Have you even seen a more delicious sight?
Than a pizza dressed up to go out at night?
Thick tomato sauce and mozzarella cheese,
Mushrooms, sausage, more peppers, please!
Onions, olives, choice pepperoni!
Anything goes, just Top it all off with
it's looking a sprinkle of spice—
Hey, who so good
took a slice?

Now it's your turn. In BOX 1, create a short concrete poem about an umbrella. To get inspired, shut your eyes and imagine that you are an umbrella. How does the rain sound? Are you soaked? Are you lonely? When you're finished, use BOX 2 to design a concrete poem in a shape you choose.

BOX 1   BOX 2

Poems will vary.

Look for other examples of concrete poems in books of poetry.

page 91

Horseplay

Why did the horse sneeze?

Decoder
4 bars .... T
6 inches ...... K
bar 5 L
bar 2 .... A
bar 6 L
2 inches ...... U
2 bars .... P
5 inches L
bar 8 .... T
7 inches ...... W
bar 3 .... O
bar 1 .... S
3 inches ...... E
8 inches C
8 bars .... M
4 inches ...... T
3 bars .... H
bar 4 .... N
bar 7 I

Answer each question about the graph. Then use the Decoder to solve the riddle by filling in the blanks at the bottom of the page.

1. Which is the tallest bar on the graph? bar 8
2. Which is the shortest bar on the graph? bar 6
3. How tall is bar 1? 3 inches
4. How much taller is bar 5 than bar 4? 4 inches
5. How much shorter is bar 4 than bar 2? 5 inches
6. How tall is bar 8? 8 inches
7. Which bar is taller: bar 1 or bar 7? bar 7
8. Which bar is shorter: bar 2 or bar 3? bar 3
9. Which bar is twice the size of bar 1? bar 5
10. How many of bar 4 would equal bar 8? 4

IT HAD A l i t t l e "c o l t"
          2 7 10 4 9 3   6 8 5 1

page 92

A Musical Lesson

There are many kinds of paragraphs. When you write a comparison paragraph, you compare by telling how things are similar and contrast by telling how things are different. You can use a Venn diagram to organize your ideas. Here is an example.

Trumpet
• brass
• has a mouthpiece
• has three valves

Both
• are played in orchestras
• musical instruments
• take practice

Violin
• wood
• four strings
• played with a bow

Complete the paragraph using details to compare and contrast the trumpet and violin. Remember to capitalize and punctuate correctly.

Trumpet Versus Violin

The trumpet and violin are both musical instruments that are _____. However, there are some important differences. The trumpet _____

On the other hand, the violin _____

Paragraphs will vary.

Both instruments _____

Make a list on a sheet of paper of things to compare and contrast such as a house and an apartment building, ice skating and skateboarding, or spinach and broccoli. Choose one pair. Make and complete a Venn diagram like the one above. Then write a paragraph to tell how they are similar and different.

Week 8

page 95

Is That a Fact?

What is the difference between a fact and an opinion? A fact can be checked or proven. An opinion is what someone believes or feels about something. An opinion cannot be proven.

Fact → Cocoa beans are used to make chocolate.
Opinion → Chocolate pudding is better than chocolate ice cream.

Read each sentence. Write F next to each fact. Write O next to each opinion.

O 1. Everyone in the world thinks chocolate makes the best candy.
F 2. In Switzerland, the average person eats about 22 pounds of chocolate in a year.
F 3. That means the Swiss eat about 160 million pounds of chocolate annually.
O 4. I think Americans eat more chocolate than that.
F 5. People also use chocolate to make drinks and to flavor recipes.
O 6. There's nothing better than a chocolate donut with chocolate glaze.

Look at the pictures. Then write two facts and two opinions about each snack food. Use clue words such as think, best, believe, like, and dislike to signal an opinion.

1. Fact: 2. Fact: 3. Fact:

Opinion: Opinion: Opinion:
        Sentences will vary.

As you listen to a conversation among your friends about an issue that is important to them, try to identify the facts and opinions you hear and write them down on a sheet of paper. Then ask, "Can this statement be proven?" If the answer is yes, then it is a fact. If not, then it is an opinion. Circle any clue words or phrases that signal opinions.

page 96

Oh, My Aching Heart!

Don't read this story yet! Give it to a partner and ask him or her to tell you the parts of speech under the blanks below. You give a word for each part of speech, and your partner writes it in the blank. Then he or she writes the words in the story and reads it aloud.

1. FRIEND'S NAME
2. PLURAL UNIT OF TIME
3. ADJECTIVE
4. VERB ENDING IN ING
5. ADJECTIVE
6. ADJECTIVE ENDING IN EST
7. BODY PART
8. CELEBRITY'S LAST NAME
9. NOUN
10. PLURAL NOUN
11. ADVERB
12. ADJECTIVE
13. ADJECTIVE ENDING IN ER
14. VERB

Dear __1__,
I have watched you from afar for many __2__ now. I can be silent no longer. The time has come to tell you how I feel. I think you're really smart and __3__. Whenever you are __4__ near me in class, I feel __5__ inside. I think you might be the __6__ person I have ever met. You are the apple of my __7__.
If you want to find out who I am, meet me at 3:30 behind Principal __8__'s office. I'll be the one wearing the __9__ on my head. Until then, please accept this bunch of __10__ as a sign of my affection.
Yours __11__,
Your __12__ admirer
P.S. It is __13__ to __14__ and lose than never to love at all.

Answers will vary.

page 97

A Smart Butterfly

When multiplying with decimals, place the decimal point in the product, counting from right to left, the same number of places as the sum of the decimal places in the factors.

$6.95   The decimal point is 2 places, counting $6.95   Place the decimal point
x 3   from right to left, in the top factor.   x 3   2 places, counting from right
        There is no decimal point in the $20.85 to left, in the product.
        bottom factor: 2 + 0 = 2

Multiply. Then use the code to answer the riddle below.

I.   E.   A.   T.   W.   O.
2.8   26.5   32.8   20.41   0.24   0.04
x 3   x 4   x 7   x 5   x 9   x 8
8.4   106.0   229.6   102.05   2.16   0.32

H.   S.   I.   T.   I.   M.
3.06   300.1   24.81   24.6   41.5   0.416
x 6   x 8   x 6   x 5   x 3   x 5
18.36   2,400.8 148.86 123.0   124.5   2.080

T.   M.   C.   A.   A.   A.
45.6   48.5   4.53   3.08   3.49   6.94
x 8   x 3   x 3   x 4   x 7   x 9
364.8   145.5   13.59   12.32   24.43   62.46

Why did the butterfly learn decimals?

I T   W A S   A
124.5 123.0   2.16 62.46 2,400.08   0.32

M O T H – E M A T I C I A N
2.080 0.32 102.05 18.36 106.0 145.5 24.43 364.8 148.86 13.59 8.4 62.46 12.32

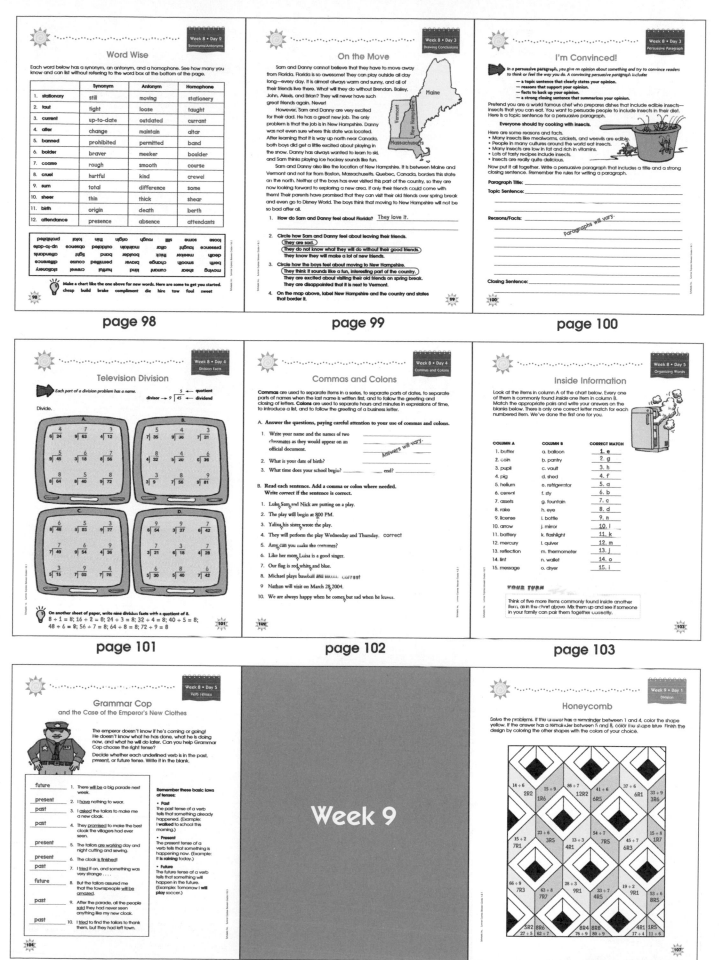

page 98

page 99

page 100

page 101

page 102

page 103

page 104

Week 9

page 107

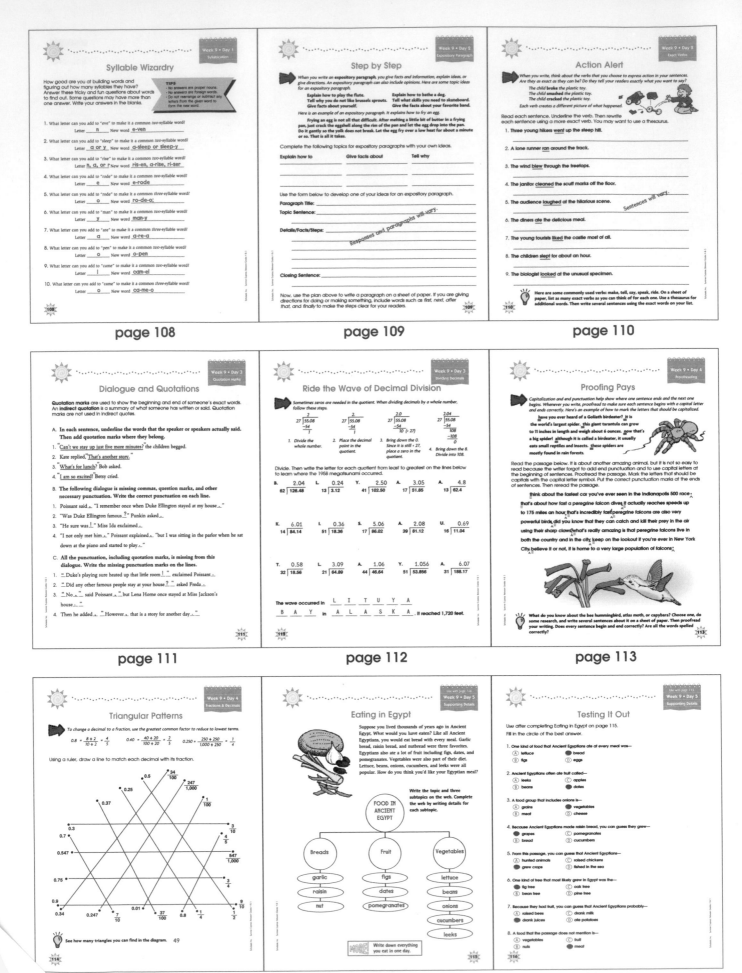

page 108

page 109

page 110

page 111

page 112

page 113

page 114

page 115

page 116

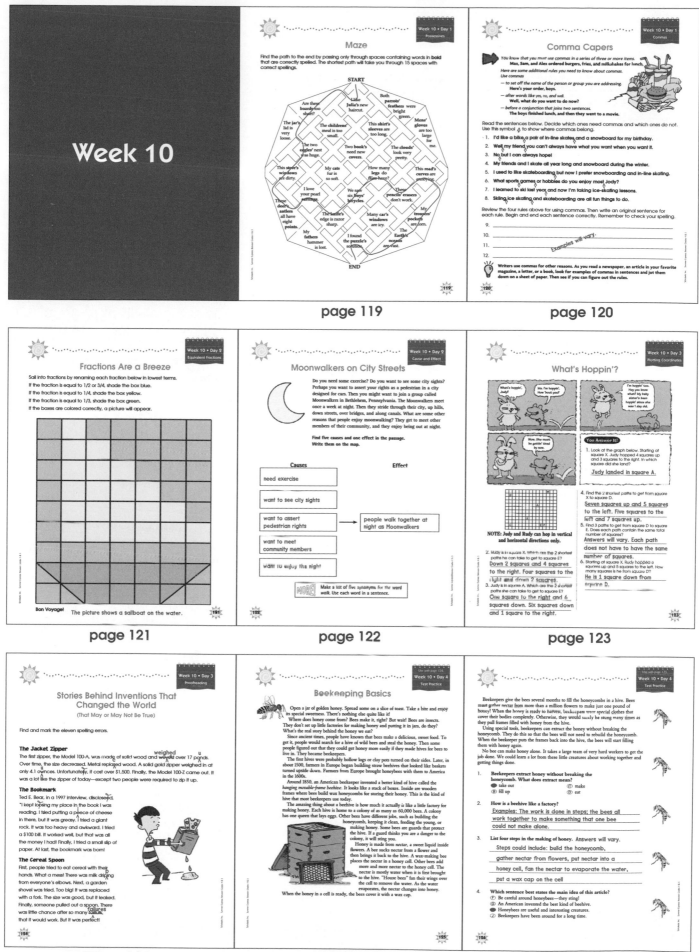

page 119

page 120

page 121

page 122

page 123

page 124

page 125

page 126

Identifying Relationships

Write the phrase from the box that tells how the first two words are related.
Then write the correct word to complete the analogy.

Relationship	Same Class Antonyms	Part/Whole Homophones	Synonyms

1. weight : wait :: gilt : ____   Relationship __homophones__
   Ⓐ wave   ● guilt   Ⓒ gill

2. work : play :: deep : ____   Relationship __antonyms__
   ● shallow   Ⓑ dive   Ⓒ job

3. elm : pine :: bee : ____   Relationship __same class__
   Ⓐ birch   Ⓑ honey   ● beetle

4. seam : seem :: I : ____   Relationship __homophones__
   Ⓐ me   ● eye   Ⓒ you

5. kernel : corn :: seed : ____   Relationship __part/whole__
   Ⓐ soil   Ⓑ water   ● watermelon

6. forest : woods :: field : ____   Relationship __synonyms__
   ● meadow   Ⓑ flower   Ⓒ farmer

7. leave : arrive :: asked : ____   Relationship __antonyms__
   Ⓐ go   ● told   Ⓒ inquired

8. wheel : we'll :: hall : ____   Relationship __homophones__
   Ⓐ help   Ⓑ hill   ● haul

Explain to someone in your family how you chose each answer.

127

Free-Throw Percents

Hoops, Dunk'n, and Shooter are on the court again! How do their numbers add up?
Follow the steps below to make sense of their percents.

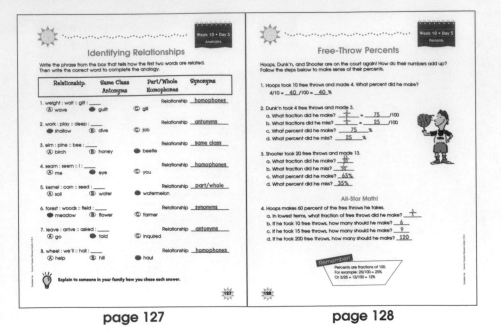

1. Hoops took 10 free throws and made 4. What percent did he make?
   4/10 = __40__/100 = __40__%

2. Dunk'n took 4 free throws and made 3.
   a. What fraction did he make? __3/4__ = __75__/100
   b. What fractions did he miss? __1/4__ = __25__/100
   c. What percent did he make? __75__%
   d. What percent did he miss? __25__%

3. Shooter took 20 free throws and made 13.
   a. What fraction did he make? __13/20__
   b. What fraction did he miss? __7/20__
   c. What percent did he make? __65%__
   d. What percent did he miss? __35%__

All-Star Math!

4. Hoops makes 60 percent of the free throws he takes.
   a. In lowest terms, what fraction of free throws did he make? __3/5__
   b. If he took 10 free throws, how many should he make? __6__
   c. If he took 15 free throws, how many should he make? __9__
   d. If he took 200 free throws, how many should he make? __120__

Remember!
Percents are fractions of 100.
For example: 25/100 = 25%
Or 3/25 = 12/100 = 12%

128

THIS CERTIFIES THAT

_____

IS NOW READY

FOR GRADE ____

CONGRATULATIONS!

I'm proud of you!

_____